THE MUMMY'S BOYS

THREATS AND MENACES FROM ULSTER'S PARAMAFIA

THE MUMMY'S BOYS

THREATS AND MENACES

FROM ULSTER'S PARAMAFIA

JIM McDOWELL

Gill & Macmillan

Gill & Macmillan Ltd
Hume Avenue, Park West, Dublin 12
with associated companies throughout the world
www.gillmacmillan.ie

© Jim McDowell 2008
978 07171 4268 2

Type design: Make Communication
Print origination by Carole Lynch
Printed and bound in the UK by CPI Mackays, Chatham ME5 8TD

This book is typeset in Linotype Minion and Neue Helvetica.

The paper used in this book comes from the wood pulp of
managed forests. For every tree felled, at least one tree is
planted, thereby renewing natural resources.

A CIP catalogue record for this book is available
from the British Library.

5 4 3 2 1

CONTENTS

INTRODUCTION

This book is about a newspaper, and the people who work on it.

'On' it, not 'for' it, because a newspaper is a living thing.

When it rolls off the presses it takes on a life of its own.

At its very core, it is about life. About people. It records for posterity their triumphs and their tragedies: from winning the Lotto, to losing their lives. It sits on the pulse beat of the country, or the community, it serves.

As I write this chapter in June 2008, I am proud, without boasting, to put it on the record that for the past four years the ultra-professional and, yes, brave staff of the *Sunday World* have won four successive newspaper awards in Northern Ireland.

That unique success, never before attained by any Sunday newspaper in Ulster, saw us lift the Sunday Newspaper of the Year title in 2004 and 2005, the overall Newspaper of the Year accolade for 2006 and the Sunday Newspaper of the Year title again in 2007.

No small achievement, given the background of threats we have received, both formal and informal, and the continuing menace and duress we work under. The threats have come from the paramilitaries in Ulster who, over the past number of years, have evolved into what we in the *Sunday World* have labelled the paraMafia.

These terror gangs were set up, allegedly, to protect their own people from the threat of pogroms and reprisals from other paramilitaries. After thirty-seven years of their squalid sectarian war, which claimed 3,289 lives on both sides of the Border, we all by now know who they are: the IRA, the UDA, the INLA, the UVF, the UFF, the RIRA, the LVF, CIRA, the Red Hand

Commando… the blood-laced, bloodlust list goes on and on and is now etched in history, and infamy.

What the *Sunday World* set out to expose, over a number of years, was that these gangs were not the protectors of their people: in fact, we reported relentlessly that they were the persecutors of their own people, leeching off them with their protection rackets, drugs and death.

This book portrays the level and nature of death threats journalists on the *Sunday World* received during those years, and continue to receive, from the paramilitaries. And we don't only bring our work home with us. We bring our threats home with us, too. All of our families know what it is like to hear a strange noise in the middle of the night, and not know what's coming to your door: or who may be battering their way through it, to harm not just us, but maybe our wives, husbands and children, too.

At the *Sunday World*, we've done some hard stories together. And covered some hard, and heart-breaking stories.

None more so than the murder of our reporter Martin O'Hagan, gunned down by the drug-dealing Godfathers of the so-called Loyalist Volunteer Force on Black Friday, the night of 28 September 2001.

The last book I wrote, *Godfathers*, was dedicated to the memory of Martin. The book was almost completed and a preface already written, when he was so callously cut down in front of, and protecting, his wife Marie.

In journalistic terms, this new book 'moves the story on'.

Godfathers covered the *Sunday World*'s, and my own personal, dealings with the paramilitary as their organisations morphed into what we termed 'the paraMafia', up until the book was published in 2001.

Godfathers charted the rise and rise of the original 'Brigadiers of Bling', Johnny 'Mad Dog' Adair and Jim 'Doris Day' Gray, and their poisoning of their communities with death, drugs and criminal graft. My colleague Hugh Jordan and his co-author David Lister of the *The Times* have since written a best-selling and meticulously researched book, *Mad Dog: The Rise and Fall of Johnny Adair and C Company*. Since then we've witnessed Gray's demise, at the hands of the son of one of his former best buddies. In the first part of this book, I look at Gray's pernicious legacy, not least to his son, Jonathan. It makes for chilling reading.

And then there's been the rise, and fall, of Adair and Gray's successors as 'Brigadiers of Bling' and drugs Godfathers, the Shoukri brothers. In Part Two of *The Mummy's Boys*, I have profiled for the first time the Shoukri brothers, primarily Andre and Ihab, but also, in passing, Yuk. Drawing on sources once close to Andre and Ihab, this book pieces together their background, upbringing and, most importantly, what turned them into the drug-dealing, drug-using, violent and, ultimately, self-destructing paraMafia Godfathers they became.

These brothers were to be the last of the UDA's 'Brigadiers of Bling', a dubious soubriquet with which the *Sunday World* had dubbed their predecessors, Adair and Gray.

The Mummy's Boys is, in part, the intriguing story of how two boys whose father came from Egypt came to be 'Brigadiers' in the biggest paramilitary organisation in Western Europe. And, in a white 'Protestant' organisation with renowned links, when it suited it, to the British National Front and other neo-Nazi parties around the world. At one stage, Andre Shoukri, later to be labelled by us as 'The Bookies' Brigadier' because of his gambling addiction, was a protégé and big buddy of Johnny 'Mad Dog' Adair, the very same man who had once fronted up a skinhead punk-style band with the rabidly racist mantra, 'There ain't no black in the Union Jack'.

We exposed the Shoukris and their ilk routinely, ruthlessly

and relentlessly in the *Sunday World*, not least because they set themselves up and styled themselves as 'paraCelebs'. The Shoukris didn't like us: and me in particular. And they let that be known very publicly, and very privately.

They, 'The Mummy's Boys', are used as a backdrop to the rest of the menaces mentioned in the pages that follow.

Some will shock you. Some will sadden you. But, at least, the sun is now, hopefully, rising on a new Northern Ireland, and a new Ireland.

And that, in the end, brings me back to what my game, journalism, is all about. There are plenty of other people in this country, North and South, who have lived through the trauma of threats, both to themselves and their families. Among them police officers, soldiers, prison officers, judges and magistrates, lawyers and many other brave folk from every walk of life who stood up to the bogeymen, either on their own doorsteps, in public, or in our, or other, newspapers.

I take my hat off to all of them. And not least to the other hacks, reporters, journalists—call us what you will—who, like ourselves, 'told it like it is', and suffered threats because of it.

Many great scribes and broadcasters have visited these shores since 1969. Many of them have won big awards for their reporting here. But like their reporting of other 'war zones', they were only in and out of here on assignment, returning to base—and their families—in safe environments.

Journalists who lived and worked here in Northern Ireland never had those kind of breaks. They were here 24/7. They faced—and still do—a constant threat. Going to work. At work. In the pub. Going home. At home.

The nature and stature of those threats could differ widely. Picking up a 'tickle' from our own sources. A direct threat down the phone from a terror gang using a codeword. An anonymous threat. Or the police visiting your workplace, or, even more disconcertingly, your home, with an official warning that terrorists were planning an attack on you, your staff, your office or, in some cases, your family.

A selection of such threats is highlighted—or 'low lighted', given the low life who issued them—in this book, in both written and documentary form. I salute all my fellow journalists who have received them, endured them, and continued to 'see the job through'. Many times they have stood by us. I also salute them for that. Many times we have stood by them too. I'm proud of that.

Newspapers are all about triumphs and tragedies, and the in-between. But once you fall in love with that living thing being printed, the rumble of the presses pulsing like rolling thunder under the very soles of your feet, the sweet scent of printers' ink pricking your senses, the headlines hurrying off the gantries at breakneck speed before your very eyes… That's *real* romance. That's the best feeling in the world. And, in spite of all the threats and menaces, that's what makes it all worthwhile.

To the staff of the *Sunday World*, who are also my friends, I dedicate this book.

And, last but by no means least, to my best friend, Lindy.

I'm proud of you all.

Jim McDowell, June 2008

PART I
THE BRIGADIERS
OF BLING

01 | THE PARAMAFIA: PART I

The threats and intimidation began long before, but reached a climax in 2003. And the person behind them? One of the first Brigadiers of Bling, Jim Gray.

The run-up to Easter 2003 had been hard: the hardest since I started in journalism, around the same time as the spark which lit the bonfire of the Troubles in 1968.

Sure, I had reported on the atrocities of the Troubles since: witnessed and chronicled the blood of good and bad men trickling down manholes after shootings and mass slaughter, and watched as slivers of people where shovelled off the streets into plastic 'forensic' bags after bombing blitzes. I'd reported on funerals, knowing that inside the coffins weights had been placed instead of bodies, to allow the victim's family to think that their loved one, however mutilated, had some dignity in death.

But 2003 was brutally hard.

The frontline loyalist paramilitaries—the UDA (allied to the Ulster Freedom Fighters, its twin organisation which used to claim its killings), the Ulster Volunteer Force, and its 'sister' wing, the even more ruthless Red Hand Commando—had issued a blanket threat against our newspaper. It covered all reporters, photographers, advertising staff, secretarial back-up, any one, in fact, connected with the *Sunday World* in Northern Ireland. Newsagents were visited by masked men with guns and told to stop selling our paper. Van drivers were stalked by terrorists and told not to deliver the paper. Bundles which the brave drivers got through were burned in the streets, or dumped in rivers. This was an attempt—ugly, upfront and blatantly undermining the rule of law—to put us off the streets for good.

All the above-named organisations were aligned to what was then called the Combined Loyalist Military Command. They issued a crude poster which was pasted up in loyalist areas. This poster alleged that our paper was attacking the Protestant community. They said that we were setting up loyalists for assassination.

Manifestly untrue, of course. We were exposing the gunmen and bombers and sectarian assassins and baseball-bat beaters and knee-cappers and the loan sharks and protection racketeers—not to mention the drugs barons—prostituting and living off the backs of their own people.

Much later, after a series of exposés of Gray and his mob, we were to discover that the spark which lit the torch for the terror campaign against us was a page-one story under the headline,

DORIS, YOU'RE DEAD!

The story, much of which now seems grimly prophetic, read:

UDA DRUG lord Jim 'Doris Day' Gray has been told to kick the drugs habit.

The Flash Harry terror boss has been handed a chilling ultimatum—get out of the drugs trade or die.

The move is part of the UDA's drive against drugs, and is being pushed by south Belfast brigadier Jackie McDonald.

McDonald is an outspoken critic of drugs and is known to have voiced his disapproval of Gray's trade during Inner Council meetings since the overthrowing of Johnny Adair's C Company.

In a dramatic fall from grace Gray is now looking at the prospect of losing his lavish lifestyle and his large cash stash.

The flamboyant terror boss now faces a life-or-death choice—quit drugs and get back in line or run the risk of assassination.

We, as reporters, had pens and pencils in our hands. The paramilitaries had guns and bombs in theirs, and blood on them.

The loyalist bogeymen labelled this a boycott. It was not. It was threat, intimidation and terror at its worst. It was an ugly, blatant and obscene attempt to gag the Press, pure and simple. It aimed to censor freedom of speech and expression.

On the mid-March Saturday morning when I first heard that the posters were being pasted up, I discovered that they were even going up in newsagents' windows. People trying to earn an honest shilling had been threatened. They had no option but to comply.

I went out into the heart of East Belfast and ripped down one of the posters. It is reproduced in this book. You can judge for yourself the level of threat pulsing off its poison prose. But we faced that down for five ferocious and fearful weeks.

The ring on my finger has an inscription: *Virtus Fortunae Comes*—Fortune Favours the Brave, the motto of my old school. It's a motto I try my best to live by. But any man or woman who says they never experience fear, for themselves, for their families or for their friends, is a liar or a fool.

There were many times when I was haunted by the question: is this really worth it? The thought of what could happen to my family, to someone on the *Sunday World* staff or to some other worker caught up in the terror campaign was constant and chilling. But while I agonised over the horrific possibilities I was also absolutely determined that we would not—that we could not—give in to terror.

And we didn't. Papers were even delivered into hardcore loyalist areas and left on the doorsteps of newsagents. On one infamous Sunday morning, a very good friend recruited one of his drivers to take a van into the heart of East Belfast. He rode 'shotgun', so to speak, with the brave driver. Of course, no gun was involved on our part, but I drove behind the van in my Jeep, and papers were delivered. They mightn't have been sold. They may have been burned or shredded by the bogeymen, but the point was, we weren't bending the knee to anyone.

And we went further. The various paramilitaries had driven a resolution through the so-called Loyalist Commission backing the 'boycott.' The Loyalist Commission was the umbrella body covering the main loyalist paramilitaries (except the Loyalist Volunteer Force, of which more later) and fronted by 'do-gooders', at least one of whom was a Unionist politician. To my mind they were misguided and duped into giving credibility to men of terror and gangsters—like Johnny Adair, Jim Gray and the Shoukris. The then Secretary of State John Reid had at one point held a meeting with the Commission.

The Chairman of that Commission was a Presbyterian Minister, the Rev. Mervyn Gibson. He had taken the cloth after serving in the RUC's Special Branch. I believe he should have known better than to allow himself to be associated in any way with this campaign of terror and intimidation. It should have gone against everything he believed in as a minister of God and a former police and anti-terrorism officer.

So I made that clear in the appropriate way. I 'splashed' with him on the front page, that is, I made him the lead story on Page 1 of the paper. We published his photograph, with the banner headline: THE MAN WHO TRIED TO GAG US. I wrote an editorial for the paper, bylined with my own name, and underlined by my position in the *Sunday World*. I was livid at the time of writing. What I wrote for the edition of 16 March 2003 highlighted, in no small way, my anger. It was short, but very much to the point.

BY JIM McDOWELL, NORTHERN EDITOR

Get off our backs!

And get off the backs of the people of this country, once and for all.

That's our message to the paramilitaries in Northern Ireland—all of them—today.

Last night, we discovered that the UFF/UDA were demanding that this newspaper should be boycotted in areas they think they control.

Posters went up, which told lies. Shopkeepers were intimidated, told not to sell this newspaper, and told they would be shot, or their businesses burned, if they did.

So much for the UFF/UDA recently announced 'ceasefire'.

So much for peace. So much for no more terrorist activity.

So much for the freedom of the Press. So much for a free society: a society free from intimidation and threat.

So much for this newspaper trying to do what it owes to this society, by exposing paramilitaries (all of them, without fear or favour), by exposing drugs pushers, by exposing paedophiles, and by supporting peace, for ALL of the decent people of this country, Protestant and Catholic.

We won't be gagged. We won't be censored. We won't be bullied.

And neither should you.

The aforementioned Rev. Mervyn Gibson may have been a clergyman, but all Hell now broke loose... I found out that a delegation from the Loyalist Commission was planning a meeting with the Chief Constable of the Police Service of Northern Ireland, Sir Hugh Orde. They were going to see him at his headquarters, Brooklyn, based in the leafy suburbs of Knock in East Belfast. I'd got the tip-off around teatime. I was still working in the office. The meeting was that very night.

As soon as I heard about it I jumped into a taxi and went straight to the gates of the Brooklyn police HQ. News and TV crews were already there. The meeting had started. I waited with the rest of the media scrum at the gates.

When Gibson and his Commission cohorts came out into the dark, chill night, it was apparent that some of the most senior representatives, mouthpieces and apologists for the UDA/UFF and UVF/Red Hand Commando were there. I waited until Gibson started talking to the cameras, giving a summary of the meeting with the Chief Constable. He was in the middle of answering the first question when I interrupted.

As the cameras rolled and the boom microphones picked me up, I asked him, point-blank, why the Commission he was representing—the main men at his elbow—were threatening the lives of *Sunday World* staff, including me. Why they were trying to silence our paper and put it off the streets?

Gibson hesitated. Ignoring me, he tried to continue his impromptu press conference with the rest of the Press pack.

I refused to let him. I asked him again why he and those with him wanted to silence the Press and censor the freedom of speech and expression which is one of the cornerstones of democracy.

He said he would be consulting his solicitor. And with that he promptly abandoned the pavement Press briefing, and stormed off towards the park where he had left his car. The paramilitary posse scurried after him. I kept badgering them as they walked, turning to face them personally, asking them to explain their so-called 'boycott' of the *Sunday World.*

If they had an answer they didn't offer it. They turned their backs on the banks of cameras and reporters and, without a word, made for their cars before slinking off into the night.

At the time I was angry and aggrieved. I was more concerned about getting answers. It was only afterwards it was pointed out to me how pathetic those so-called big men, the paramilitary bosses, had looked as they fled to their cars pursued by a solitary hack. And that particular confrontation was of course, recorded for posterity.

I went to Barney O'Neill's pub for a pint when I got back into Belfast city centre. To be honest, I needed one. The punters in the bar had seen the TV footage, and as I walked in, the banter was fierce: 'McDowell, we're amazed you're still alive. We always knew you were mad—but not that fuckin' mad!'

The truth is, I was mad. But mad in the angry sense. I was sick of the constant, relentless threats. And there was to be no let-up, as I found out after another no-punches-pulled editorial in the following weekend's paper.

I had asked for, and received, the TV news footage of my head-to-head with the delegation from the Loyalist Commission outside police headquarters. I lifted a still photograph from that and wrote:

SPECIAL REPORT: BY JIM McDOWELL, NORTHERN EDITOR

This was the moment of truth for the Loyalist Commission.

It occurred minutes after their hour-long meeting with PSNI Chief Constable Hugh Orde at his Knock HQ in East Belfast last Thursday night.

The Commission had 'endorsed', to use chairman the Rev. Mervyn Gibson's word, a boycott of this newspaper...

Now, if people want to boycott this newspaper—because we publish the truth: and sometimes it hurts—that's up to them.

This is a free society. People should be free to say, to write, to read and to do what they wish (as long as it's inside the law).

That means that if you don't like a newspaper, you don't have to buy it. And the same goes for television—if you don't like what's on, you switch it off.

But by the time of their meeting with the Chief Constable on Thursday night (those who had called for the boycott) had moved outside the law...

There was widespread intimidation. People connected with this newspaper were threatened, either directly, or indirectly.

That's why I went to speak to nine members of the Loyalist Commission last Thursday night.

They refused to talk to me.

Well, here's the deal.

Why don't you start talking—instead of walking?

This newspaper and myself have never bent the knee to paramilitaries of any hue. We're not starting now.

But what we are prepared to do is open the door. And if that means meeting out of the public gaze, away from the glare of TV cameras, so be it.

You can tell us what you think of this newspaper. But, in turn, we reserve the right to publish, without fear of censorship, and without threat or intimidation.

We do not believe that what you have embarked upon helps the loyalist position.

The veteran and respected Unionist politician and peer, Lord Laird of Artigavan, has gone on the record to call what is happening 'a disgrace'.

Lord Laird has appealed to the Commission to rethink its position.

We endorse his wise counsel.

He said: 'You must have a free Press. The media is entitled to report inside certain parameters. But if you think the media does not understand your case, the problem is yours.'

He added: 'We have to get the boycott stopped.'

Referring to threats and intimidation, he said: 'It is a disgrace. I am very sorry for Jim McDowell.'

All the political parties have echoed Lord Laird's comments.

The politicians and the people are united in their condemnation of this boycott, and what it has entailed.

Their message is clear: 'We wholeheartedly support the *Sunday World*.'

As Northern Editor of this paper, I am proud to say I come from a loyalist background: from Donegall Pass, in Belfast. I'm proud of the decent people I grew up with, and I'm proud of all the decent people of this country, both Protestant and Catholic, nationalist and loyalist.

So here's our position.

We'll talk to anyone genuinely interested in creating a new Northern Ireland.

And if the Loyalist Commission are genuinely interested in that ideal—they, too, should talk—and, unlike last Thursday night, now walk.

———

On a dark night the following week, the knock came to the door, half an hour before midnight.

I told my two boys to go to the back of the house and went to the front door myself. First, though, I checked the cctv monitors inside the house, scanning all eight security cameras necklacing the perimeter, to check that our late-night caller wasn't a gunman or bomber.

It was a senior anti-terror squad officer in plain clothes. I knew him well—I'd had an off-duty pint with him on a few occasions. I let him in. He came into our living room.

I told my sons to stay where they were in the kitchen.

'Where's Lindy?' the detective asked.

Lindy, my wife, is a columnist with the *Belfast Telegraph*.

'She's upstairs. She's got an early start in the *Tele* tomorrow morning,' I replied.

'Tell her I need to talk to her too,' said the officer.

Lindy had heard him come into the house and was coming down the stairs anyway. When we were both in the living room, the detective said bluntly: 'You need to get out of the country with the boys for a while.'

I asked him why. He said: 'Jim Gray is standing at this minute in his bar planning to have you killed.' Gray had bought the Avenue One on the Newtownards Road, in East Belfast, with the proceeds of drugs and protection rackets.

The Branch man told me: 'Gray's orders to the foot soldiers are that if any of your family gets in the way, they're to be shot, too.'

I asked the senior cop—a top man at his job who had faced down terrorists and their threats over three decades—how he knew.

I should have known better.

'One of my boys is standing in his bar listening to him,' he said. One of his 'boys' was an informer, a tout in his own ranks—but Jim Gray, then UDA Brigadier for East Belfast, and since murdered by his own, didn't know it.

I told the senior policeman I was reluctant to go. I said that, like him, I'd never run away from any of them, and didn't intend to start. My wife, Lindy—who regularly pummelled the paramilitaries in print, too—felt the same way. But always, the family has to come first, and the man standing in front of us made clear our boys were at serious risk, too.

His advice was to get out of the country for a fortnight 'to let things cool off.'

We took it. We left for America the next day. But it was by no means a holiday. I was up and on the phone back to the office every morning at 5 a.m.

We've an old saying in the *Sunday World* in the Belfast vernacular. Actually, it's a song. And it goes:

> 'Oh, we're not bate yet,
> No we're not bate yet,
> No we're not bate yet,
> No, No…'

Well, we weren't bate—beaten—then. We were eventually to beat that so-called 'boycott', and another engineered by the Shoukri Brothers, a couple of years later in the summer of 2005, before they were eventually booted out of the UDA, just like Jim Gray.

In the end, neither the 'boycotts' nor the threat of the bullet or bomb stopped us. We never stepped back. As for the bogeymen who were on our backs, many of them have ended up behind bars (like the Shoukris) or buried (like Gray). And we're still here, doing our jobs on The People's Paper. Telling the people what the politicians, propagandists and especially the paraMafia, don't want them to know.

02 | THE PARAMAFIA: PART II

Jim 'Doris Day' Gray wasn't the first of the loyalist paraMafia. But he *was* the first 'Brigadier of Bling' the paramilitary prima donnas of the UDA, drugs Godfathers married to violence and crime. These 'Brigadiers of Bling' flaunted their flamboyant, Mafia-financed lifestyles: flash women, flash cars, flash hairstyles, flash Caribbean cruise holidays. They flashed big money at the bookies. In short, they were real Flash Harrys. But it was the flash jewellery that earned them the 'Brigadiers of Bling' tag.

Many of them strutted about, bodybuilding macho men, pumping iron in the gym, pumping steroids into their arms and legs—and anywhere else—to 'bulk up' their bodies. The musclebound look was then offset with ostentatious jewellery: gold necklaces dangling on their bulging chests, gold bracelets drooping from their thick wrists, gold earrings (thick as curtain rings) hanging from the sides of their perma-tanned heads.

The steroids and other drugs made them rave—and rant. The bling made them figures of ridicule. 'The bigger the

Brigadier's earrings,' went the saying in Belfast amongst the security forces and even the paramilitary foot-soldiers, 'the smaller the brain…'

But that wasn't entirely accurate. In *Godfathers*, when I charted the rise, fall and ultimate violent deaths of independent drugs godfathers like Mickey Mooney, Brendan 'Speedy' Fegan, 'Big Edd' McCoy, Frankie 'Boogaloo' Mulholland, Paul 'King Coke' Daly, and the first godmother of the drugs underworld in Ireland, ex-porn queen Nuella Fitchie—I pointed out that to run such a criminal trade, you had to be street savvy, *big* time.

Many of these people had sharp business brains. Had they been in commerce or industry, their business acumen, their cunning, would have stood them in good stead. After all, they were operating teams of 'donkeys'—runners dealing and delivering their drugs—getting the revenue back in, and then recycling it to finance huge drugs purchases which could run to a quarter of a million quid.

Jim Gray was certainly doing that. He had a team of runners working out of two bars he and his business partner, Gary Matthews, another UDA 'heavy', owned in the heart of loyalist East Belfast, the Avenue One bar on the lower Newtownards Road, and the Bunch of Grapes at the corner of the Beersbridge Road, about half a mile away.

The Avenue One, now demolished, stood just across the road from the UDA's 'Freedom Corner'—a spectacular row of wall murals lauding the UDA and its youth wing.

The runners, or 'donkeys', all wore 'bling', too. Gray's followers were known as 'The Spice Boys'.

Gray himself cut an unlikely figure in the paramilitary ranks. A hulk of a man, he earned his 'Doris Day' nickname from his beach-boy-style blond hair—all his own, not bleached. He was said to be a very good golfer. Some who knew him maintain he could have made a career as a professional in the sport.

His ex-wife, Anne, who now uses her maiden name of Tedford, once told me, 'He played off scratch when he was younger. He was offered the chance to go professional. I told him: "Go for it." But he wouldn't do it because we were about to get married. However, he was runner-up in the Ulster Amateur Championship at one stage—to winner Ronan Rafferty [later to make a major mark in professional golf, both as a player, and now, as a TV commentator on the game].

'He knew Ronan Rafferty at that stage from playing in various tournaments. Once, we went to Portmarnock to watch the Irish Open. As we walked round the golf course, half of the players there, and many of the officials, knew Jim Gray.'

That was way back then. And, of course, Gray was to turn out anything other than your regular golf club player, or patron. But it's probably where his penchant for wearing outlandish clothes started. Golfers, on the course at any rate, are renowned for their Technicolor attire. But sporting a range of garish outfits, which included his favourite pink and lemon sweaters draped casually over his shoulders, he attracted derision from the media and from the public alike. Even Johnny Adair was moved at one point to say he found Gray's dress sense 'embarrassing.' Coming from Johnny, whose own crimes against fashion were manifold, that was some insult.

Anne Tedford stuck being married to Gray for just four tempestuous years. She recalled, 'After a few years, I just said to him "I'm out—I'm not living like this". I stuck it for four years. That was enough.' She told Gray: 'See the man that I married—that's not the Jim Gray that's running about now.'

Anne grew increasingly contemptuous of Gray's mode of dress as he rose up the ranks of the UDA. She told me, 'His brain has been eaten away with drugs. Why else would he dress in pink and lemon jumpers? Look at that ridiculous blond hair.

Look at the size of him. He's ugly and he's fat. The only thing that he's got going for him is that fantastic suntan…'

Perhaps because of his penchant for colourful sweaters and, in summer, what Belfast folk call 'Miami Sammy' floral-patterned pink shirts, rumours abounded that Gray was gay or bisexual. Nothing unique there in the paramilitary ranks, of course. But compared to the macho image of old, Jim's flamboyant wardrobe was certainly entirely different.

What wasn't different was the power he wielded. His followers—mostly young, impressionable and easily led—fawned over him.

And feared him.

A notorious coke-head, Gray's temper and volcano-like volatility were legendary. His 'Spice Boys' obeyed his orders because they were too terrified not to. That's why when I was told that he'd ordered his foot soldiers to shoot me, I took it very seriously indeed. What Gray demanded, Gray got.

Even his own son, Jonathan, became a drug-using Spice Boy—tragically despite the pleas of his mother, Anne. Indeed, it was when Jonathan was born at the Ulster Hospital in Dundonald that Gray was recruited into the UDA.

Gary Matthews was to become Gray's biggest buddy, 'business' associate and mentor in the ranks of the East Belfast UDA. While Gray was still alive, Anne Tedford told me: 'Gray goes back a long time with Matthews. They met after I gave birth to our son, Jonathan, in (the Ulster) Hospital. Matthews' wife was in having a baby at the same time. Both the sons were born on the same night, 31 December 1982.

'After visiting me one night, Jim gave Matthews, who he'd never known before, a lift down the road. Matthews had said he was going for the bus. That's when he became involved in the UDA. Matthews made him the Provost Marshal. That meant he was in charge of beatings. But when he first told me this, I nearly wet myself laughing. I asked him: "Is your head cut?" But that was big dopey Jim.'

However, Anne was soon to realise that being married to 'big dopey Jim' was no joke. The good times started to roll. But not for her.

The drugs regime started by Johnny 'Mad Dog' Adair and his notorious 2nd Battalion C Company of the UDA across the River Lagan on Belfast's lower Shankill Road had begun to seep into other UDA/UFF 'turfs': most markedly into the East and North Belfast Brigades'.

Gray and Matthews began to run a criminal, and drugs, empire from the two bars they owned. After all, a paramilitary organisation with many young men in its ranks and huge tracts of them unemployed in blighted working-class areas—was custom made for exploitation by drugs barons.

One of Gray's former 'Spice Boys', now living in exile in England, recalls: 'I was just out of school at sixteen, and on the broo [the dole]. My Da had worked in the Harland and Wolff shipyard on the doorstep of where we lived in Dee Street, East Belfast.

'I would have gone in there as an apprentice, too. But by the late eighties and throughout the nineties, the shipyard was sinking: fast. There was no future for it. And no future in it for me. Also, sectarian and street violence was still rife. So I was recruited into the UDA—I thought, to fight the IRA.

'But it wasn't long before I was also recruited into Gray's drugs racket. After all, I was lifting £26 a week on the dole, in unemployment benefit. He was offering his "runners" £100 a trip to deliver drugs in a taxi to clubs or pubs where dealers were waiting—often doormen with direct links into the UDA.

'That was a huge amount of money for an out-of-work sixteen-year-old to be picking up—not only once, but twice, or three times a week.

'Soon, I was dealing myself. And getting a lot more than that in commission from Gray.'

But then, says the ex-Spice Boy, he had too much money to spend on drink. So he started on drugs himself. Just like Gray, who moved from dealing in 'blow' (cannabis) and Ecstasy tablets (E tabs) into cocaine. Gray eventually became hooked on the white powder known on the streets as 'snow'. And that was eventually to prove his downfall with the UDA.

But it was also to lead to the downfall, and death, of his own son, Jonathan.

Jonathan was just sixteen years of age when he teamed up with his father in the dangerous drugs and UDA underworld. His mother, Anne ruefully recalls, 'Up until then, my Jonathan was a good boy. He came from a working-class background, all right, but he was clever. He passed the eleven-plus examination to qualify for grammar school. And he went to a good school, the Royal Belfast Academical Institution.'

Known as 'Inst' in Belfast, RBAI has an excellent academic record, and is one of the big rugby schools in Ireland, regularly contesting the Ulster Schools' Cup Final on St Patrick's Day and supplying a star-studded stream of players to the Ulster Schools, Ulster and Irish international squads.

However, Jonathan wasn't big into sport at Inst. One of his former teachers recalls: 'He was a quiet, withdrawn lad, positive in class, and he had a good academic career in front of him.'

The 'quiet, withdrawn lad' was to change when he hooked up with his flamboyant, coke-snorting, bling-king Dad. Said his mother, Anne: 'His Da, damn him, coaxed and encouraged Jonathan to pull out of Inst at sixteen years of age. He was besotted with his Da. I tried to dissuade him. I told him the flash suits, the flash clothes, the cruise-ship holidays to the Caribbean and his father's trips to Thailand to hook up with hookers was all wrong. I told him the money his father was making from drugs was the Devil's money. But he wouldn't listen. He didn't heed my advice…'

Not heeding his mother's advice cost Jonathan his life.

Now, in Anne Tedford's neat ground-floor apartment—she still lives in East Belfast—she has only her memories of a son she adored but could not save. Memories and a few precious, framed photos.

But in all of these photographs, one man is cut out. Her ex-husband, Jim 'Doris Day' Gray. She cut him out of the photographs, just like she cut him out of her life after four years of marriage. And she is frank about the reason.

As 'big, dopey Jim' rose through the ranks of the UDA eventually to become Brigadier, she says, she 'simply couldn't live with the evil he was up to'.

03 | LIKE FATHER, LIKE SON

The taxi driver didn't want to be identified. Terrified and still traumatised, he was talking to me the morning after he picked up a double fare, two boys, one he knew, the other he didn't, outside the Avenue One bar in East Belfast.

'I pulled up outside the pub. There were two teenage boys there. They were well dressed, in clubbing clothes. One of them was carrying a leather briefcase. They got into the back of my cab. I knew the reputation of the Avenue One, but the taxi firm I was working for—well, if they had refused to pick up from the bar, they wouldn't have been in business too long. The depot would have been torched, or a driver shot dead.

'As it was, last night, these two boys were only into the back of the car when one of them pulled a gun. He put it to the back of my head, and told me to drive to a nightclub in Belfast, close to the docks. I thought I was a dead man driving.'

Taxi drivers had been 'easy targets' during the Troubles. Scores of them were among those killed during what was, in essence, a dirty little sectarian war—in spite of the rhetoric from both republican and loyalist camps claiming that it was 'ideologically driven'.

The paramilitaries on both sides, the self-styled and self-proclaimed 'protectors of the people', spawned as they were in working-class areas like the Shankill and the Falls, persecuted, preyed upon, prostituted and executed their own people. Some ninety-three per cent of the victims of the Troubles were working class. And the Provos killed more Catholics than the so-called 'Protestant' paramilitaries—their religious affiliation a misnomer if ever there was one: the vast majority of them had never darkened the door of a church, Protestant or any other, since childhood.

But that terrified taxi driver wasn't thinking about church the night he picked up those two boys. He was more worried about getting a bullet in the back of his head. So he complied with the gunman's request.

'No problem, boss,' he told him.

The nightclub he was told to drive to was just over the Queen's Bridge spanning the River Lagan running through Belfast, marrying the East—Jim 'Doris Day' Gray's turf—to the South, West and North.

'The journey took less than ten minutes,' the driver told me, 'but it was the longest ten minutes of my life…' He said the sweat was billowing down his back. 'My shirt was soaked by the time I arrived at the nightclub door.'

The two boys got out. One went into the club, taking the briefcase with him. 'He just breezed past the bouncers, who seemed to know him,' recalled the cabbie. 'He came back out about three minutes later. The gunman had stayed in the back of my taxi. There was no briefcase this time. The gunman then told me to drive straight back to the Avenue One bar. I did as I was told. When we got back to the bar, I breathed a sigh of relief as both fares got out.

'But then I was in for another shock. I thought: "They're going to let me go. They haven't even asked my religion".'

In fact, the driver was a Catholic—which had he picked up UDA gunmen in the really bad old days of the Troubles, would have been his passport to an early grave in Belfast's Catholic Milltown cemetery.

But instead of a bullet, the driver got a 'shock' financial fillip. He explained: 'One of the pair came to the passenger window. But instead of producing the weapon, as I feared, he pulled out a wad of notes. He handed the bankroll to me. He told me: "Take this. You've never seen us. You don't know us. You'll never see us again. Thanks".'

The driver took the hard cash after his hard experience and drove off. Once he got into a 'safe' area, he pulled over. He counted the notes. A cool two hundred quid for what amounted to a twenty-three-minute job.

Almost a tenner a minute.

And the point the driver was making to me the next morning, after his nightmare experience? Gray's drugs runner, the one with briefcase full of drugs to be delivered to the nightclub was, in Belfast street parlance, Gray's own 'Paris bun', his own son, Jonathan.

The taxi driver claimed that he had had 'clocked' him, recognised him. But he didn't want me to write the story at the time. Instead, he wanted me to know as 'insurance'. Just in case the gunman and Jonathan Gray had a change of heart about having let him go the previous night.

'If anything should happen to me—after all, neither of them were wearing masks, they were bare-faced,' the cabbie noted, 'I just want you to know who did it. Then, at least, there may be some sort of justice…'

The cabbie survived. Less than a year later however, young Jonathan Gray, lured into a life of drug-taking by his Godfather father, was less lucky.

To be fair, his mother, Anne, has always maintained that Jonathan was not a drug-dealer. In fact, she had a barney with me when I wrote that he was a drugs runner for his Da. She said that after Jonathan left the Royal Belfast Academical Institution (he'd got an 'A' grade in the 11-plus to get into 'Inst') and left her home at fifteen to go and live with his father, she counselled him: 'See, drugs—don't go anywhere near them. If there's a parcel, and somebody asks you to take it somewhere for them, don't.'

She told me that she warned him 'over and over again.' She told me to my face when we met after I wrote the article: 'In spite of what you wrote in the paper last week, my Jonathan was not a drug-dealer.'

But in 2002, aged just nineteen, he was to die in squalor, overdosed on a cocktail of drugs and surrounded by hookers in a hotel in the Thai sex capital, Bangkok.

Even worse, his Da, 'big dopey Jim', was in another hotel in the Thai capital allegedly engaging in gay sex with rent boys. He, too, was high on drugs: 'with more snow up his nose than you'd find in the Alps in winter' according to one source.

Knowing 'Doris Day's' history with women—he fathered Jonathan and had at least one other love child by one of a string of different women—I am sceptical about the Thai 'rent-boy'/homosexual claims that surfaced after his own death.

Still, Gray tried to blame everybody else for his son's sudden, and so premature, demise.

Court documents and statements made to the Thai police, which I later saw, claimed that there were three other boys in the room with Jonathan Gray when he died. Two of them had to flee the country after his funeral back home. Another ended up in a mental ward: and even then, Gray got his mob to fake up a car as a taxi, to try to get into the hospital to shoot that lad dead.

In Thailand, shortly after Jonathan's death, he had flown into a drug-induced rage and torn up that teenager's passport. Gray's team had then abandoned the youth in Bangkok. He eventually had to be brought home by the British Consulate. But, even then, Gray and his mob relentlessly threatened and intimidated him, sending him spiralling into a nervous breakdown and mental illness.

What Gray was attempting with the bullying cover-up was to hide his own criminal negligence as a father. While still in Thailand, he had Johnny 'Mad Dog' Adair's right-hand man and Mafia-style consigliere John White, ring and threaten me. White's nickname was 'Coco', because of his unfortunate resemblance to the famous clown.

'Don't you or your paper start writing anything bad about this wee lad,' White warned me.

I told him what to do with himself. We would write what we wanted—when we found out the truth. I told him we weren't in the business of dancing on any 'wee lad's' grave: no matter who his Da was. But we were in the business of reporting the truth.

And the truth wasn't long in getting out.

Gray had tried to sell a second dummy: getting his cronies to put out the line that he had been in Belfast at the time of his son's demise, and that he was flying out to bring the body home.

That was a lie. He was in Thailand when his only son died, in another hotel, but close by. And what he couldn't face up to was that he, and he alone, was the author of his only son's tragic destiny.

The person who told me that, who revealed the whole truth about how her son died was Jonathan's mum, and Gray's ex-wife, Anne Tedford. 'Gray made a big play in the Press of flying out to Thailand after Jonathan died. But he was in a nearby hotel the night Jonathan died, him and Murphy [William James 'Spud' Murphy, a sidekick of Gray's who bizarrely dressed in almost matching outfits to his boss]. That was all a pack of lies about him having to fly there to bring Jonathan's body home.

'But when he came home he hadn't the balls to come and tell me my son was dead. He hadn't the balls to come and face me and tell me what really happened…'

But 'what really happened' was detailed in documents drawn up by the Royal Thai police, and later obtained from them—after a three-year struggle—by British Embassy sources in Bangkok.

The main evidence came from two of the local hookers Jonathan and his mates had met in a lap-dancing club, the Baby-a-Go-Go Bar in South Pattaya. The prostitutes were twenty-five-year-old Miss Nhu-lamoon Pone-Tan, and Miss Sangwan Pra-dabphol, the same age as Jonathan Gray when he died, just nineteen. Both provided statements to Royal Thai Police Major Preecha Samrit the day after Jonathan died.

This is how the statement of Miss Sangwan, made to police on 13 March 2002, started:

> Major Preecha Samrit: 'Could you give me details of the incident?'
> Miss Sangwan: 'On 11 March 2002, at around 23.00 hours, Mr Jonathan Gray et al [sic], four persons all together, purchased four charges to take me and some other girls, four persons all together, out from a bar named Baby-a-Go-Go. Then they took us to (the) Mister Mac Hotel, Room 309. We arrived at the said room about 01.00 Hours of 12 March 2002.'

The statement goes on to say that there were three other boys from Belfast in the room.

When asked in the formal police interview what happened in Room 309 that fateful night, she replied: 'A while after we arrived at the room, Mr Jonathan and friends took out some marijuana and took it together. Mr Jonathan and his friends invited me and my friends to join them, but we refused.'

It becomes clear from the statement that the four lads were not getting a big enough 'high' from the 'blow'. So they switched to something stronger, and something which proved, in Jonathan James Gray's case, to be lethal. Miss Sangwan told the Thai cops: 'After taking the marijuana for a while, Mr Jonathan and friends jointly took the said narcotics by consumption.' The 'said narcotics' was heroin.

The hooker's statement revealed: 'They divided the white powder [heroin] into four equal heaps, then they rolled bank notes in cylinder shape and used them to sniff the said white powder into their noses. Mr Jonathan and friends, four persons all together, took the narcotics, but I and my friends, who are Thai women, did not join them.'

The other prostitute present said that was because they were Buddhists. Miss Sangwan, in her sworn statement, described to police how Jonathan began to look sick and about to vomit. She said the other males in the room, 'looked generally like those who take narcotics. Jonathan started to have convulsions,' she told the Major. 'I and my friends were frightened, but did not know the cause.'

Then comes the damning indictment of Jim Gray, and his refusal to answer an sos call to rush to the aid of his son. It also gave the lie, once and for all, to Gray's claim that he was back home in Belfast at the time of Jonathan's death, and had to fly out to Thailand to bring his body home.

Her on-the-record statement revealed: 'Until 0.700 hours of 12 March 2002, Mr Jonathan's condition was not getting better at all as he just lied [sic] in bed. I then telephoned Jonathan's father to inform him.'

Jim Gray did not respond to the sos call, even as his own son lay in his death throes in a hotel just minutes away.

Miss Sangwan said in her statement: 'Later, about 0.800 hours, an ambulance came to take Mr Jonathan from the room. So I asked to return to my place.'

The ambulance rushed Jonathan Gray from the Mister Mac Hotel on the Phra Tamnak Road in Bangkok to the Pattaya International Hospital in the city's Banglamoon District. But there was nothing the Accident and Emergency doctors there could do for him. He was pronounced dead, lying on a 'patient's bed' according to the Royal Thai police documents, at 9.20 a.m. the same morning.

In a story we carried on 19 June 2005, Jonathan's mother, Anne Tedford, said: 'I'm disgusted. How could a father do this to his only son?'

Even after Jonathan's death, there came another agonising blow to add to his mother's grief. Gray tried to ban Anne from even seeing her own son in his coffin. She had a heart-breaking, agonising and long wait before she eventually did. She told me: 'After Jonathan died, I was allowed to see him for just two minutes. His body in lay in his coffin in his grandfather Gray's house [the house outside of which Jim Gray was later to be shot dead]. At one stage, a phone call was made to my house. A woman said, "You tell Anne to come down now because we're putting the lid on Jonathan's coffin." This was because Jonathan's grandfather said that he couldn't bear looking at Jonathan in that state any more. He said if the lid wasn't put on the coffin, he was leaving the house and not coming back.

'I hurried to that house, on the basis that if I didn't see him, I still wouldn't believe that my son was dead. I saw Jonathan for all of two minutes. He was all bloated. I could only tell him by his eyebrows. He had beautiful eyebrows, like my own. That's all I recognised him by.

'It broke my heart. But to this day,' says Jonathan's mum, 'as far as I am concerned, that was not my son in that coffin.'

Worse followed for Anne when Brigadier of Bling Jim Gray was himself shot dead. Anne had been adamant that Gray was not to be buried in 'my Jonathan's grave' at Roselawn, Belfast's sprawling municipal cemetery on the eastern outskirts of the city.

Many loyalist godfathers and foot soldiers are buried in that graveyard—a large number of them, like Gray, victims of their one-time comrades.

Anne Tedford, of course, was not invited to—and had no intention of attending—her ex-husband's funeral. She only found out afterwards, much to her distress, that her pleas had been ignored.

The father—the Godfather—of the drugs racket in East Belfast was now lying beside the son he'd sucked into the evil trade. Posthumously posturing as his son's Guardian Angel? More accurately, his son's Angel of Death.

04 | THE ANGEL OF DEATH

There was another internal victim of Gray's East-Belfast UDA mob who was also visited by the Angel of Death.

This man was once one of Gray's commanders in the UDA/UFF in the heart of the working-class part of the city, an area flanking the once-famous Harland & Wolff shipyard where the *Titanic* was built, and skirting the Oval soccer ground, home to one of the city's 'Big Two' football clubs, Glentoran.

The name of that one-time UDA 'heavy' was Geordie Legge.

Legge met a horrible fate in a so-called 'Romper Room' in the back lounge of one of the two pubs Gray and Gary Matthews ran: the Bunch of Grapes, at the junction of the Castlereagh and Beersbridge Roads in the area known as Ballymacarrett.

The UDA had long used what were colloquially known as 'Romper Rooms'. Taking their name, in sick humour, from a children's TV show from the 70s, they were in reality torture chambers, often at the back of paramilitary shebeens, where victims were 'rompered'—beaten, tortured, mutilated, stabbed and ultimately killed.

Some of the worst excesses of the Troubles were committed in such dark and Satanic dens. And innocent women victims were no exception. Two of the most infamous 'Romper Room' murders claimed the lives of women—innocent, vulnerable women, victims of mistaken identity: their sectarian killers thought they were Catholics. The UDA murdered a mother, Ann Ogilby, in a 'Romper Room' in South Belfast in July 1974. Heartrendingly, her young daughter stood outside the door crying, listening to her mother's screams as she was bludgeoned to death.

Twenty years later, in 1994, The Red Hand Commando, an even more ruthless wing of the Ulster Volunteer Force, killed an epileptic girl, Margaret Wright, in an appalling act of savagery in a converted bookmakers which had been turned into another loyalist shebeen. That murder scene, with dark irony, was called The Bad Bet band hall. Obscenely and inhumanely, the thirty-one-year-old's body was dumped in a plastic wheelie bin in what is known in Belfast as an 'entry', an alleyway, where such bins are normally left out for the City Council's refuse collection.

The disposal of the bodies of their victims was always a problem for the killers. Some corpses were carried out and put in the boots of cars. Sometimes, the cars would be burnt with the bodies still inside. At other times, the remains of the murder victims would be dumped well away from the scene of their killing.

Such was the case with thirty-seven-year-old Geordie Legge from Island Street in the east of the city. He got a terrible beating in the back lounge of the Bunch of Grapes. Hardened detectives reckoned the horror show lasted for hours on end. Then the former commander was subjected to a multiple stabbing. Finally, his throat was cut. His blood-soaked body was then wrapped up in the filthy carpet which had covered the floor of the pub lounge. (There was a wheelie-bin angle to this murder, too. It later transpired that the blood-soaked carpet from the Bunch of Grapes pub where Legge was tortured and almost decapitated was taken to the back of Gray's other bar, the Avenue One, put in a big industrial metal wheelie bin and set on fire, in an unsuccessful attempt to destroy vital forensic evidence. Murder detectives later found the charred carpet but no one was ever charged with or convicted of the gruesome Legge murder).

After his cruel torture and killing, Geordie Legge's body was ferried in the boot of a car, wrapped up in the carpet, to a skinny wee road high up on the plateau of the Castlereagh Hills which tower over East Belfast. The rollercoaster of a road where the burly UDA 'hard man's' body was dumped, close to a barred gate to a field, is called the Clontanacally Road. That was Geordie Legge's last-but-one resting place—before he was buried by his family at nearby Roselawn Municipal Cemetery.

The mutilated corpse had been discovered early on a Saturday afternoon in January 2001, dumped on the green verge at the side of the tarmac. By that stage, myself and our chief crime reporter, Hugh Jordan, had almost wound up work for the week. We had a good 'sleeper' story—a backgrounder which no one else had—ready to splash on the front page, and we'd written it up that morning. So the paper, barring any bombs blowing up, or bullets flying, or any other atrocity, was ready to go to bed.

We headed to watch a rugby match at Malone Rugby Club, fortuitously, as it turned out, also in East Belfast. It was there we met a senior cop we both knew: a good big lad. We had just watched a superb try being scored, when the police officer finished a call on his mobile phone. He turned to us. 'Lads,' says he, 'is the paper away, or are you still working?'

'We're still on the job,' says I.

'Well,' says the policeman, 'if I were you two I'd get yourselves up to the Clontanacally Road.'

Luckily, we hadn't even had a sip out of the two pints we had in our hands. We jumped back in the car, and headed to where the cop had told us.

Part of the road was taped and cordoned off. The rest of the Press pack were starting to arrive. I alerted our subs, who were making up the pages, and told them a fresh story was breaking.

The police already had a scene-of-crime tent over the body. White-suited forensic detectives were poring over the death scene. A police photographer was at work flashing off pictures of the body under the canvas.

Eventually, there was a briefing. But at that stage the police did not know the identity of the victim. And, as a steer, they let it be known that he was so badly mutilated that he was going to be very difficult to identify. However, they already had a hunch that the murder was drugs related.

Geordie Legge was a big fella, well-known for being able to 'handle himself': in other words, he was a street fighter. But there was another 'big fella' who at that time lived close to where the body had been dumped. This man had been close to Ulster's first drugs Godfather, Mickey Mooney, who had been the first victim of the Provo hit team Direct Action Against Drugs (DAAD), in the 18 Steps bar in downtown Belfast early on the Friday evening of 29 April 1995.

His killers shot Mickey 'Moneybags' Mooney in the back of the head as he stood answering a call on a public phone in the pub. They had to. 'Moneybags' was no mug when it came to shooters. A diminutive, muscle-packed ex-boxer, he had once toured Belfast's Golden Mile of packed pubs and clubs threatening doormen not to 'interfere' with his drug-dealing operation.

He backed the threat by wearing an overcoat with one of the pockets cut out. Where the pocket used to be, Mickey Mooney carried an Uzi submachine gun. If a bouncer didn't immediately get his point, Mooney swung open the coat and pointed the snub-nosed Uzi at the doorman. The 'point', in more ways than one, was usually taken…

In stark contrast, the guy who had been close to Mooney was a big, almost obscenely obese, lumbering man mountain. Not connected to any paramilitaries, nonetheless, DAAD gunmen, posing as window cleaners, had once tried to murder him in his own heavily fortified home, close to where Legge's body had been dumped.

In spite of what had happened to his friend and mentor Mickey, this boy lusted after money from the drugs trade, too. But he certainly chickened out the time he and his 'minder' tried to threaten me. I had just finished an off-the-record meeting with two members of the Drugs Squad at the time. I was driving home when this man and his 'minder'—a drugs 'heavy' later shot dead himself—spotted me in my car on Belfast's Ormeau Road. They U-turned and started tailing me. They made it *very* obvious, even though I'd clocked them the minute they made the U-turn.

I allowed them to follow me close to my home. Then I sped into a labyrinth of neighbouring streets. I knew my way around. My pursuer and his bouncer mate didn't, so I lost them easily. Then I drove home and parked my car well out of the road.

I then walked back to a pub near my house. As I walked, I phoned my two Drugs-Squad contacts on my mobile, filling them in on the boys stalking me. I told them where I was going. I went down to the pub and planted myself at the perimeter wall, right out on the street. I knew that this guy and his minder would be circling, looking for me.

Eventually, they pulled on to the main road where I was standing, my oul' baldy head standing out like a lighthouse without the lamps on. They drew up to the pavement, the minder in the passenger seat closest to me.

I knew the main man wouldn't have the balls to do anything. He can't fight, anyway. So I went over to the passenger side door. The other Aughnacloy—boy—I knew could handle himself. So I lifted my foot and put it against the car door so he couldn't get out.

He wound down the window. 'Lookin' for me?' I asked into the minder's ugly mug.

And just at that precise moment, as they say in all the best crime novels, a car pulled up behind the drug-dealers, bumper-to-bumper. And out clambered my two contacts from the Drugs Squad. 'Like a bat out of Hell' goes nowhere near describing their flight from the scene. Only thing was, he almost took the leg with which I'd been pinning the door closed with him... But myself and the two Drugs Squad cops had a good laugh at that.

My stalker lived at the time in a two-storey house, heavily fortified downstairs, with him living upstairs... just in case. And now, only a couple of miles away, an unidentified body was lying under that police scene-of-crime tent on the Clontanacally Road.

As the rest of the Press pack departed, a detective asked Hugh Jordan and myself to remain behind. The forensic photographers had been using, among their specialist soco cameras, a Polaroid camera which produced instant prints. They asked if we would mind having a look at them, as with the mask of blood and multiple stab wounds, it was difficult even to make out the murder victim's face, or any distinguishing features on it. They thought it might be Mickey Mooney's one-time buddy.

It was a horrendous sight, even more so as we were standing only a few feet away from where the body was still lying. But we told the police we didn't think it was Mooney's ex-legman. After all, we'd confronted him and another sidekick, an ex-Irish National Liberation Army terrorist, as they'd arrived back into Dublin airport from Amsterdam once after another drug-buying mission, and we'd been threatened face-to-face. 'Don't you put our f*****g pictures in that f*****g rag of yours,' the overweight 'heavy' threatened as his minder circled us menacingly.

''Course not,' I replied, as our staff photographer stood behind a pillar in the airport terminal, snapping away. The pair were prize exhibits in the *Sunday World* two days later. On the front page, as the splash.

We were pretty sure now that it wasn't the main man of that pair on the Clontanacally Road. But that left both us, and the police, in a quandary. And it meant the rest of the rugby match was off, for us, anyway.

Changing the paper's front page was on, definitely, from the 'sleeper' splash to this freshly breaking murder story. We started working the mobiles. And we hit pay dirt—or in this case, grave dirt—with one of our loyalist contacts. He told us of rumours in East Belfast that a senior UDA man had been missing from his home for a significant amount of time: so significant, in fact, that his family had begun to get anxious for his safety: 'very anxious', as the source put it.

So we headed for the man who knew East Belfast like the back of a Red Hand of Ulster, never mind his own hand, Davy Ervine, the former convicted UVF bomber who was, in turn, the guiding hand in turning that terror organisation towards politics. In the process, he became a highly respectable (and much respected, on both sides of the Irish Border) Belfast City Councillor and Stormont Assemblyman for his party, the Progressive Unionist Party, the political wing of the UVF.

David and I had gone head-to-head on many occasions,

when he, his Party, or the UVF, didn't particularly like what we were reporting about them in the paper. But our meetings would always end in a pint. Once, Ervine had intervened in a meeting I'd had with loyalist terrorist Billy Wright with the pithy words, 'What are you doing with that headcase?' Wright was still in the UVF at the time, before he was booted out to set up the murdering machine which was the LVF. He had been trying to impose a death threat on everyone who worked for the *Sunday World*, and the newsagents who sold it, using the thumbprint of the UVF.

I had gone head-to-head with Wright over the threat, telling him what I thought of him. But when Davy Ervine caught sight of both of us, he was, characteristically, as sharp as one of the Stanley knives he once used serving his time as a carpet fitter way back in his youth. 'Headcase' was the cut-to-the-bone word he used to describe Wright: and to his face, too. And Wright just walked on by…

That was the kind of forthrightness, and courage, which was David Ervine's hallmark: in politics, and in life.

David Ervine tragically died in the intensive care unit of Belfast's Royal Victoria Hospital after suffering a heart attack and complications on Monday 8 January 2007. His funeral took place, with Sinn Féin President Gerry Adams in attendance, in the heart of the Protestant, loyalist Newtownards Road, a sight I never thought I'd witness.

Yep, I met Davy Ervine in a variety of places. And I always knew where to find him on a Saturday. In the Raven Club on Belfast's Castlereagh Street, where his Glentoran Supporters' Club met, where he could always have a pint in peace, and from where it wasn't too far to walk to the 'cream cookies'—the bookies—to have a punt on a horse, or two, or three…

When we arrived, Davy took us over into a corner of the club. We explained the background. 'Aye,' he said, 'I've heard a top UDA man is missing. Give me a minute or two to make a couple of phone calls,' he added.

We knew he had the best network of loyalist—and other—sources of anybody in East Belfast, be they paramilitary or politician. He was back to us within about three minutes. 'It's Geordie Legge,' he confirmed.

By that time, it was getting dark. But we'd found out where Geordie Legge lived—*had* lived. We went to the street. Two detectives had arrived just before us and were getting out of their unmarked police car as we drew up. That was the corroboration we needed, if any.

We watched them go into the house. We couldn't go and knock at the door. That would have been too dangerous at such a tinderbox time in this fiercely loyalist area. But we waited for the detectives to come back out of the house. When they did, I asked one of them if that was Geordie Legge's house. She said nothing.

That was total confirmation. They wouldn't have been there if it had not been him.

We scurried back to the office, wrote up the story, and switched the splash. And we pointed the finger at the person we thought responsible, the first 'Brigadier of Bling', Jim 'Doris Day' Gray.

The paper was only on the streets for a few hours the next day when the phone rang. Another death threat…

05 | KILLER COUPS

The word on the street was that Geordie Legge had been 'done in'—because he had 'done in' £30,000 of Gray's drugs money.

Legge had allegedly been in charge of Doris's drugs operation in the huge, sprawling Braniel housing estate perched on the flanks of the Castlereagh Hills. One theory was that he had coined the ill-gotten gains from the drugs racket and then trousered thirty grand of it which should have gone into the coffers of Gray and his gang. Never mind that Gray himself was blowing thousands of pounds, meant to go into central UDA coffers, to finance his growing cocaine habit.

As it turned out, the Legge 'embezzlement' line was just another piece of black propaganda put out by Gray and his acolytes, just like the line that he'd been in Belfast when his son Jonathan had died in that Bangkok hotel bedroom. In fact, we discovered later, Geordie Legge had been plotting a coup against Gray. He planned to shoot him dead.

Like a lot of other veteran UDA men in East Belfast, Legge thought that Gray's drugs habit—and his drugs empire—were running out of control, and that his activities went against every alleged 'principle' on which the UDA was founded. In the eyes of those 'oul' timers', they had joined up to protect the Protestant working-class people; now, they realised that criminals like Gray were exploiting and prostituting those same people. And poisoning their young people with drugs.

So Legge was plotting the first, internal, bid on Gray's life. But he made a fatal mistake. He confided in someone else that he planned to shoot Gray in his own pub, the Avenue One. And the confidante Legge trusted Judassed him, touting on the coup plot to Jim Gray. And that's why he was 'Romper Roomed'—kidnapped, tortured, had his throat cut and killed.

A source deep inside Gray's East Belfast Battalion at the time later told me: 'It's true that Legge had done in drugs money due to go to the UFF. The figure of thirty thousand was being bandied about. But Legge was a hard man himself. He was reputed to be a killer. And it would have taken a hard man to take him down.

'That's why a gang had to do it: Gray's gang. But it wasn't over the drugs money. It was because Legge was plotting to murder Gray. One of Gray's "entourage"—one of his closest aides—was in on it, but he hadn't the balls to follow it through. He chickened out. He squealed to Gray. He told Gray exactly what Geordie Legge was planning for him.

'Legge was plotting to do Gray in. He had the gun and all for the job. He wanted to take over from Gray. That is why he himself was murdered. But he himself was a killer. The likes of him then, they were all killers.'

In this context, he mentions one name in particular, but it isn't Jim Gray's. And I have been able to find no sources who have ever said that Jim Gray was a killer himself, although he was definitely an accomplice in the brutal slaying of Geordie Legge.

However, I got one revealing insight into Gray's status as a 'hard man' from none other than his ex-wife, Anne. While he was still living, I asked her about his reputation. I told her I'd heard he once jumped out of a car and 'beat the s**t' out of Michael Stone before Stone committed the Milltown cemetery murders.

The brave woman who had once walked out on the self-styled Brigadier of Bling confirmed that, while he might have made a great golfer, he would never have made it as a boxer. 'He can't fight. I could beat Jim Gray in a one-to-one fight.'

It is now a matter of record that a coup of a different kind—orchestrated by the Inner Council of the UDA—also proved to be the *coup de grace* for Gray himself. The UDA Inner Council—and their overall boss, Jackie McDonald, Brigadier for South Belfast (and golfing companion of Irish President Mary McAleese's husband, Martin, at the exclusive K Club in Co. Kildare)—had had enough of the Brigadiers of Bling. McDonald and other senior Inner Council members wanted to hoover the organisation over a process of years: they wanted drugs, protection rackets, loan sharking and other crimes vacuumed off the streets and binned. In return, they wanted money from the British Government: but more of that later.

To this effect, by February 2003 they had already ostracised, and then exiled, Johnny 'Mad Dog' Adair, his wife Gina (dubbed 'Mad Bitch'), and their drug-dealing son, Jonathan (aka 'Mad Pup') from Belfast's Shankill Road.

Jim Gray had a hand in that, too. The row that really sparked Adair's exit from UDA ranks—and Ulster—started, intriguingly, over, of all things, an ice-cream van.

Adair and his Mafia-style consigliere, John 'Coco' White, were already in big trouble with the ruling Inner Council. They had triggered internecine feuds with the Ulster Volunteer

Force. In one such vendetta, nine lives were blown away on both sides in the space of just two months. Plus, Adair's drugs-dealing empire was running out of control. And what 'Mad Dog' and his team were up to was bringing too much heat on to the rest of the organisation.

In other words, the cops were not just putting the bite on 'Mad Dog', they were snapping at the heels of the rest of the organisation, too. And Adair was just too 'up front', appearing at Orange parade flashpoints like Drumcree with his snarling Alsatian dog, Rebel, (he thought that was funny: he named it Rebel because it had come from a Catholic home), and hogging the headlines as often as possible.

He revelled—and 'Rebelled'—in the publicity.

In short, Adair had become not only a paramilitary: but what we in the *Sunday World* dubbed a paraCelebrity. His antics made daily news reports and had become as compulsive viewing for some as reality TV shows like *Big Brother*.

McDonald and his, majority, core support on the Inner Council didn't want that. They wanted the whole organisation to go low profile and low key.

Adair wasn't dancing—and wouldn't dance—to the same schmaltzy tune, however. He and his sidekick 'Coco' White travelled the two miles from the lower Shankill over the River Lagan to Gray's turf of East Belfast for an Inner-Council meeting. There, a huge row erupted over drugs. Adair and White were told in no uncertain terms that their drugs empire, based on the lower Shankill, just half a mile from the front gates of Belfast City Hall, had to be run down and folded up. Adair bitterly pointed out that Gray was still running his huge drugs racket: and that Gray was 'half out of his head most of the time anyway on f*****g cocaine.'

Adair railed at the accusation that he and his mob—as reported in the *Sunday World*—were selling drugs to school kids. 'For f***'s sake,' snarled Mad Dog, pointing at Gray sitting there in a bright lemon cashmere sweater, 'he's flogging f*****g E-tabs and blow to primary school kids in Ballybeen out of the back of an ice-cream van!'

'E-tabs' are, of course, Ecstacy tablets; 'blow', cannabis. Ballybeen and Tullycarnet are twin, massive loyalist housing estates sitting far out on the outskirts of East Belfast, flanking the dual carriageway from Belfast to Newtownards. I have had many letters on my desk from distraught mothers there pleading with the *Sunday World* to keep exposing Gray and his drug-dealers for 'poisoning our kids'. 'Please get the monkeys off our backs,' was the common theme of decent parents there.

But that bellowing blow-up from Adair at the Inner Council proved to be his last, defiant stand against the mainstream UDA who now wanted to disown him. Soon after, he was back behind bars for breaching the licence which had allowed him out of jail early under the terms of the Good Friday Agreement in 1998. McDonald's mainstream then seized the opportunity to move against his mob and his family on the lower Shankill, forcing over four dozen of them to flee the country by high-speed ferry. Sneeringly the once powerful C Company were now referred to as 'Seacat' Company.

But what Adair had angrily alleged about Gray had been noted—*big* time—by the other Inner-Council brigadiers present. One source told us the next day: 'They were appalled. Not only were they starting to move to put the knackers on UDA drug-dealers selling the stuff to adults. But now, they'd discovered that Gray had stooped so low as to allow his mob to be selling drugs to primary school kids... from an ice-cream van!'

As Gray left the meeting that night, he realised Adair was done for, but he also realised he was in deep trouble himself. A close confidante of Doris's later told me: 'Gray could feel the chill of the eyes on him as he left the room. The atmosphere was colder than… well, the freezer of an ice-cream van.'

It was from that moment that Jim 'Doris Day' Gray knew that, in UDA circles at any rate, he was well and truly licked. And it was then that he decided on his own coup, but it would be unlike Geordie Legge's failed assassination coup on him. Instead, he would stage a coup against the rest of other five brigades of the UDA in Ulster. He would break away from the mainstream UDA and form a rebel Brigade in East Belfast, running it as his own, separate and annexed, criminal empire: the same would happen with the South-East Antrim Brigade a few years later, in 2007, under their drug-dealing brigadier, Gary Fisher, and his front man, Tommy 'Millions' Kirkham.

But Gray had been snorting too much snow up his nose. 'The cocaine has him living in cloud cuckoo land,' observed a veteran UDA man. And there were many like him who were absolutely scunnered (sickened) with Gray's movie-star lifestyle: the Caribbean cruises, the sun- smack- and sex-trips to Thailand, the flash cars, the five-star hotels, the luxury apartments he was living in some of Belfast city's most salubrious districts.

Gray, in his drug-deluded state, thought he could take the whole of the East Belfast Brigade with him. But there were many old-timers who baulked at such a parasitical prospect. Behind Gray's back, they were talking to McDonald and to the rest of the Inner Council, filling them in on the coup that was being planned. So the Inner Council decided to fill Gray in as well: to stand him down as Brigadier and expel him.

They summoned him to a court-martial, and they did so with some panache: the court-martial was to be held… in Gray's own pub, the Avenue One. But the star turn didn't turn up for his own show, or showdown. As one Inner-Council brigadier later put it in street parlance: 'He didn't have the balls.' In gentler language, he didn't have the courage. Instead, he turned to coke.

'He was out of his head the night the Inner Council held their meeting. Gray didn't show. They court-martialled him anyway,' a senior source who was at the meeting reported.

And the 'crime' Gray was found guilty of in his absence? The same as Geordie Legge's: plotting a coup. And he was similarly 'convicted' of the crime for which he'd passed the death sentence on Geordie Legge. In the UDA's handbook, this amounted to one word. Treason.

As they say, 'What goes around, comes around.' In Gray's case—like many others in the UDA, IRA, UVF, and INLA before him—what was to come around after him being found guilty of 'treason' was a round: a round from a gun that is.

But before that happened, Gray tried one last throw of the dice. The Saturday after he was court-martialled and expelled from the UDA, he tried to rally what he thought was left of his 'troops'. A meeting was called for the Bunch of Grapes bar, owned jointly by Gray and Gary Matthews. Its purpose was to give two fingers to the ruling Inner Council, to show 'solidarity' with 'Doris', and to set up a breakaway Battalion from the mainstream, with Gray still at its head.

That same night, a UDA source who was summoned to the meeting, arranged to meet me. He revealed: 'I got a phone call that there's rumblings in the Bunch. I was told to get there. I went down. I saw Murph, [William James 'Spud' Murphy, one of Gray's top henchmen, and one of the three, with Gray and Gary 'Mackers' Matthews stood down simultaneously by the Inner Council]. He told me: "Big Jim's on his way down. Everybody's been told. They are to be here to show solidarity and support."'

My source told me the idea was that with the backing of the mob expected to turn up, Murphy and Matthews would go to the Inner Council to plead the case for Gray and themselves. But the former hierarchy of the East Belfast UDA were in for a shock. Said my source: 'Only five "heavies" were there: Murphy and Matthews, Matthews' two sons, and Stuarty Charlesworth. The rest were only kids. Teenagers and school kids.

'There were only a few BMWs about. Another "Beamer" suddenly arrived. A big fellow wearing a baseball cap and a white shirt got out and came into the Bunch. The guy standing beside me said: "That's him." I said I doubted it. I said Gray would never wear a baseball cap, because it would wreck his hair!

'But it was him. That showed how much pressure he thought he was under: that the UDA might try to kill him. But it was a poor attempt at disguise.

'However, when he came inside, Gary Matthews met him face-to-face. He told him: "No harm to you, Jim, but if this is all the support you can muster up, you're on your own. How are we going to plead with or take on and square up to the Inner Council with just a bunch of school kids backing us?" With that, Matthews shook his hand and left, taking his two sons with him...'

The end for one Brigadier of Bling was nigh: in more ways than one.

Oh, and there's one footnote—or foot-in-mouth-note—to finally add here. At the Inner-Council meeting just three nights earlier, where Gray had been court-martialled, the five other brigadiers present were asked to vote for his expulsion on the count of treason. There were no votes against. But another 'Brigadier of Bling', the not-long-appointed brigadier for North Belfast, abstained. His name, none other than Andre Shoukri.

When I reported that, accurately, having been fed from a source very close to the Inner Council, in the following Sunday's paper, I was to get a phone call from the Bookie's Brigadier himself.

And yet another threat.

Jim Gray, court-martialled, expelled and with the charge of 'treason' hanging over him, knew his card was marked and his time limited. The cops were closing in, as was Northern Ireland's Assets Recovery Agency—the equivalent to the Criminal Assets Bureau in the Republic of Ireland—who would later sequester Gray's assets. He was worried about going to jail, and even his one-time closest cronies doubted if Gray, used to winging it away on exotic holidays and feathering his own nest, could 'do bird' behind bars.

What's more, if Gray was indeed, as had long been suspected, singing like a canary as a police informer, he was going to be 'dundered', in Belfast street parlance, by one of his own: shot dead, in other words.

He had obviously tippled to this, so it came as no surprise when, in April 2005, just a month after he'd been expelled from the UDA, he tried to do a runner, ironically, over the border, heading for Dublin to get a flight out of the country. The old loyalist mantra about how 'we will never forsake the blue skies of Ulster for the grey mists of an Irish Republic' obviously didn't carry much weight with the departing Doris!

That loyalist slogan had first emerged during the signing of the Ulster Covenant by Sir Edward Carson's anti-Home Rule protestors outside Belfast City Hall in 1912. Dramatically, many of them had signed that Covenant in their own blood. Shortly after his aborted bolt for the border, Gray was to pay for his past, dying in a pool of his own blood.

Gray was stopped by cops in his souped-up Mini Cooper heading south on the dual carriageway at Loughbrickland in County Down.

Ironically, for a supposed 'loyalist' paramilitary boss, Loughbrickland has heavy resonance in loyalist history. It is where Prince William of Orange, King Billy, stopped to muster his troops on his way to the Battle of the Boyne to take on his father-in-law, James 1, in 1690. And it is where one of the first Orange Lodges was formed.

After being stopped with several thousand in cash and a money order for £10,000 in his possession, Gray ended up lodged in jail after that April Fool's dash of 2005. As police investigations continued in the North, a number of properties were raided and thousands of documents seized.

At street level in Belfast the talk was inevitably that Gray was squealing. At a court appearance in September where he was charged with money laundering, Gray claimed the money had come from the sale of his two pubs (the Avenue One was demolished as part of a major redevelopment project in East Belfast). He was released on bail and went to live in his father's house in the working-class, mainly Protestant Clarawood estate in East Belfast, less than a quarter of a mile from where he used to live in a luxury apartment in upper-class Cherryvalley, about which the raucous Ulster comedian James Young used to banter that 'the women there wear fur coats—and no knickers!'

But there was nothing comic about the murder of Jim 'Doris Day' Gray on the night of 4 October 2005.

Gray had asked a close buddy of very long standing to deliver a set of weights to his father's home so that he could work out. He had reportedly started a new fitness regime, kicking the drugs habit and getting himself into some sort of shape because he thought he was going to prison. He knew he might face hard times in there at the hands of other loyalist paramilitary inmates, especially since he had been court-martialled. Indeed, it was expected that Gray might have to spend his time behind bars in special protective custody, if not in solitary confinement, for his own safety. So he was attuning himself to going behind iron bars, by starting to pump iron.

However, when his very close accomplice delivered the weights, he also delivered death.

This friend had two other people with him, at least one of whom was his own son. As Gray came out of the house and went to help unload the barbells, his long-time business associate and mate turned Judas. He turned to Gray, offered his hand, and as both shook hands, he said, 'Sorry about this, mate...'

As he spoke, two gunmen stepped up behind 'Doris' and delivered a sudden, and brutal, *coup de grace*.

At the time, speculation immediately sparked that it was the UDA, headed up by Jackie McDonald, which had ordered the very public execution of Gray in the street outside his father's house. I was later to learn that the Judas had, in fact, acted without the sanction of the UDA or its Inner Council. Said one source who knew him as long as Gray had: 'The Judas himself was in the bad books of the UDA at the time. He had been one of those who had turned up at the Bunch of Grapes pub the Saturday that Gray had called the rally... Gray trusted this man implicitly. But when he brought death to the doorstep of where Gray was then living, Jim Gray literally didn't see it coming.'

As it turned out, the execution of Gray didn't get the Judas, his son, or the second gunman back into the good books of the UDA. At the time of writing, more than two years after the assassination, all three are still in 'limbo land' as far as the mainstream, ruling Inner Council of the organisation is concerned.

At the time, though, the cold-blooded killing sparked a firestorm of speculation about 'Whodunnit'. And the Sunday after the murder, we reported a fire of another kind. I got a tip-off that wood had been collected and piled into a bonfire in the loyalist housing estate of Tullycarnet. The UDA were, and still are, strong in this huge working-class housing complex on the way out to Ulster's only ice rink, the Ice Bowl at Dundonald on the eastern outskirts of Belfast.

The UDA in Tullycarnet would once have been warm towards Gray, but it was in housing estates like this that his dealers had been selling E tabs to kids, as Johnny 'Mad Dog' Adair had snarled at him at that acrimonious Inner-Council meeting in the Avenue One Bar.

By the time of his spine-chilling murder, the UDA in Tullycarnet had turned ice-cold on Jim Gray. Which is why the wood for the bonfire had been collected. The Saturday night after his killing, there was to be a street party to celebrate the demise of the demoted and disowned paraMafia boss known as 'Doris Day'. I went out with a photographer to take a picture of the pyre on which an effigy of Gray was to be burned. A placard stuck on the pile of wood on that Saturday afternoon already read: ROAST IN HELL, GRAY.

We splashed on the front page the next morning with the picture story, under the headline BONFIRE OF HATE. We weren't gloating, although Gray had given my staff, and me in particular, such a hard time over all the years, fanning the flames of hate against us. Now, we were merely trying to show how fickle fate could be, how dramatically the spiral of the bullet could turn in paramilitary circles.

After all, as I've already reported, we in the *Sunday World* had been the victims of a vicious campaign of hate, masquerading as a 'boycott', instigated at Gray's behest by the so-called Loyalist Commission and the Combined Loyalist Military Command in March 2003. Much later we were to discover that the spark which lit the torch for Grey's terror campaign against us was our DORIS, YOU'RE DEAD story, in which we revealed that Gray was to be kicked out of the UDA.

The UDA vehemently denied we were right back then: hence the life-threatening 'boycott', which Gray spearheaded to the extent of wanting me shot dead.

Considering what history has recorded since—and I say this

without gloating, for I have always believed the place for para-military crime lords and criminals is behind bars, not executed and incarcerated in coffins—we were right back then. We consistently exposed Gray as a Godfather of crime. The UDA tried to pillory and punish us for it, but eventually even they copped on to Gray—and court-martialled the crime lord.

We certainly stand vindicated now.

PART II
THE MUMMY'S BOYS

06 | THE SOPRANO

The original 'Brigadiers of Bling'—first, Adair, then Gray —set the template for The Mummy's Boys, Andre and Ihab Shoukri, who followed in their footsteps.

The Shoukri brothers had seen how two relatively young men (Adair is still only 42, Gray was assassinated when he was 47) had used the UDA to set up and run criminal empires in West and East Belfast respectively. With the demise of the 'Bacardi Brigadier' Jim Simpson, thus called because of his fondness for Bacardi rum, they saw, and seized, their chance.

Simpson had been stood down and exiled from the UDA hotbed in Tiger's Bay where he lived, after the Inner Council, spurred on by Adair, moved against him. For Adair it was the ideal opportunity to elevate his protégé Andre Shoukri, still only in his early twenties, into a position of real power.

The catalyst for the Inner-Council move had been street violence ordered by Simpson which had resulted in the death of a sixteen-year-old schoolboy. From a pub 'patronised' by paramilitaries, close to the interface with the Catholic New Lodge Road, Simpson had ordered members of the UYM—the

Ulster Young Militants (the youth wing of the UDA)—in his area to spark a riot with their republican counterparts just 500 metres away in the New Lodge District. Other young people, on both sides, became embroiled. The street disturbance that night in November 2001 became bloody and vicious.

Simpson, as brigadier for the area, was sitting half-pissed in The Mount when he ordered pipebombs on to the street. Now, pipebombs are crude devices—as the name suggests, lengths of lead or metal stuffed with explosives. Sometimes the contents of fireworks are siphoned out and poured into the metal pipes. Rudimentary as they are, when lit by a fuse, they can turn into lethal homemade grenades, which fragment on impact. A local policeman in the area described them at the time as the weapons of 'garden-shed terrorism'.

And that night one of them turned out to be a lethal weapon. A Protestant teenager, Glen Branagh, among those ordered on to the street by Simpson, was standing close to a pipe bomb just before it went off, prematurely. It blew half his head off.

In the aftermath of the boy's death local UDA men were to claim that the device had been thrown into the Protestant crowd by republican youths. But police chiefs maintained that this was not the case.

What was not a matter of argument was that UDA bosses were now furious with Simpson. Not only had he failed to 'lead from the front' in the street battle that he had ordered. He'd been in his customary haunt, glugging Bacardi rum as 'the action', as it turned out, deadly action, unfolded in the street just yards away. The UDA hierarchy had had enough. Simpson was stood down, court-martialled and ordered out of the country.

He fled to Scotland. And that was the signal for the Shoukris to step into the void.

Even though the elevation of Andre Shoukri had been pushed by Adair, ironically, in 2002, Andre Shoukri had been sent to shoot Johnny Adair during an internal UDA feud! (Shoukri may once have been Adair's protégé from their time together in prison, but when 'Mad Dog's' C Company on the Shankill went head-to-head with the powerful South-East Antrim Brigade, who were backed by the rest of the Inner Council, Shoukri knew that there was only going to be one winner— and it wasn't going to be his old jail buddy.) Mysteriously, the cops stopped the car Shoukri was travelling in on the outskirts of Rathcoole, North Belfast, where he had gone to pick up the weapon to do the job. He had this weapon with him in the car.

Even more mysteriously, Shoukri, a known paramilitary terror boss, eventually got off a lengthy prison sentence of six years: on the basis that he was carrying that gun for his own protection! He got just two years instead.

Two factors come into play here, and both later surfaced from members of the North Belfast UDA Brigade who were in the ranks when Shoukri was Brigadier of North Belfast. One, he alerted the police himself the day he was due to shoot Adair, because he either didn't want to do the job, or because he believed Adair would shoot him dead instead. Two, he got off the possession-of-a-weapon rap because he was, and still is, a police tout, an informer.

That whole Adair murder-bid balls-up didn't go down well with the UDA hierarchy, all of whom had been at the Inner Council meeting where Gray was court-martialled and Shoukri abstained. The Inner Council had long memories, and, when Shoukri, too, was eventually expelled, just like Jim Gray before him, it was simply playing catch-up, a classic case of 'Lest We Forget.' When it came Andre Shoukri's time to get dumped, the Inner Council didn't: forget, that is.

But all that was to come. In the years between 2003 and 2006 Andre Shoukri and his brother, Ihab were to use the UDA as a front for their huge drugs empire. Like many paramilitary leaders they wrapped the flag of loyalism around them. But their cause was primarily their own pockets. They became paramilitary parasites, plundering their own community in North Belfast, inflicting misery and suffering upon the decent working-class Protestant people in the areas they 'controlled', through protection rackets, drugs and other gangster activities.

Eventually though, these two prime examples of the ParaMafia thought they had grown powerful enough to plunder their own terror organisation. Their greed was to be their downfall.

At the *Sunday World*, we worked hard to expose the activities of the ParaMafia and the Shoukris in particular and to reveal just how much havoc they were wreaking on their own community. Andre Shoukri, the younger of the two brothers—thirty-one at the time of writing—was accorded another dubious title by the *Sunday World,* that of the 'Bookies' Brigadier'. Flush with the his ParaMafia mob's cash, he would develop a runaway gambling addiction. One estimate reckoned he placed an astonishing £884,000 on the noses of racehorses in just one year. That was a graphic reflection of just how much money the Shoukris' criminal empire was raking in; in just one area of Belfast, the 'turf' of the North Belfast Brigade.

I was told by some in his own camp that there were times that his blood boiled so much at that soubriquet, he was fit to jump over Beecher's Brook at the British Grand National to get at me. So enraged did Andre become, that he tried to engineer a 'meeting' with me. It was an invitation I declined—as I will explain in full later—for a very good reason. To 'give me the message'. To try to intimidate me.

Yes, the Mummy's Boys, the Shoukris, were a constant menace

to me and to the staff of the *Sunday World* who did so much to expose them as shysters, gangsters, and drugs Godfathers. Nonetheless, I have a confession to make. I may have had a part to play in saving Andre's life.

At one stage, when Andre had risen through the UDA ranks, his mother, Katie, was tending to the terminally ill on a daily basis in the Northern Ireland Hospice on Belfast's Somerton Road, not far from the family home on the Westland housing estate.

I was tipped off that an IRA intelligence unit, based in the Provo stronghold of the New Lodge Road, situated not much more than half a mile from the Hospice, was monitoring Andre Shoukri's movements. They'd 'clocked' him going to visit his mother in the Hospice on a regular basis.

Now, because we have lived through, and reported, Ulster's terror war, we at the *Sunday World* have a clear code of conduct. We don't believe that any story is worth a life. It was a 'given', and still is, that if we come across any information which may save a life—no matter whose life that is, paramilitary, politician, policeman, or a lay person in the street—we do something about it. We either tell the police, or we get word to the person whose life we believe is in danger.

That was the case with Andre Shoukri. I got a third party to contact a senior figure in the UDA, a man straddling both the military and political wings. Shoukri got the message. He stopped visiting the Hospice. The Provos missed their man.

Now, there are some people—maybe a lot—who will say that was not a model thing for me to do, but I've already put down the marker: no story is worth a life, and if we can prevent the taking of life, no matter whose, we will.

———

But let's begin at the beginning.

The Shoukri brothers were no strangers to crime. They had been hoods from an early age. There are those now—even those who 'served' with them in UDA ranks—who insist they would always have turned out crime kings, a north-Belfast version of the Kray twins in East London. But that needn't have been the case for all three boys, all of whom had good educations at a couple of Belfast's best schools in terms of both sporting and academic attainment.

All three are the sons of an Egyptian father—a Coptic Christian seaman who settled in Belfast after marrying their mother, a local girl. The father was killed in a road accident in France when Ihab, Andre and the third brother Yehia, known as Yuk, were still young.

Their mother Katie was, and still is, a devoutly Christian woman who devotes a lot of her time to helping terminally ill folk. Still, when her husband was so suddenly taken away from her and her family, Katie Shoukri found it hard, like many single parents, to bring up her boys.

Incredibly as it may seem for these half-Egyptian boys who later joined a 'Protestant' paramilitary organisation, Katie started bringing up her sons in New Barnsley in West Belfast! It had once been part of a housing experiment on the lower slopes of the Black Mountain, overlooking Belfast. Protestant and Catholic families moving out of the Falls and Shankill Roads were meant to live together. But as the Troubles unravelled from street protest into bombs, bullets and savage sectarian murder, Protestants either fled or were forced to abandon the integrated housing 'experiment'. Still, Katie clung on as long as possible, as that's where her mother, Rossi, lived.

One-time family friends say that relatives of the boys' father back in Egypt wanted to take them to grow up there. They say that at the time, there was talk of some kind of 'inheritance' which would go to them if they returned to the land of their father. But Katie Shoukri wanted to keep her brood in Belfast, so the story goes, and the right to any family 'inheritance' was forfeited. And that meant Katie was out working: she had to be to clothe and feed her sons, and she needed her mother to help look after them.

Indeed, when their grandmother died, the UDA negotiated an arrangement with the Provos, now in control in New Barnsley, a temporary 'truce' whereby Andre, Ihab and Yuk were guaranteed 'safe passage' back into the estate to pay their last respects, if not to attend her funeral in public.

However, while the boys were still young, Katie had to move them. They moved a couple of miles away into the fiercely loyalist Benview housing estate off Belfast's Ballysillan Road. The estate was a breeding ground for loyalist paramilitaries, the UDA, the Ulster Volunteer Force—later, the Loyalist Volunteer Force—and other splinter guerrilla groupings like the Orange Volunteers. In their ranks in those days there were not only sectarian bigots, but racists. Some elements within the UDA maintained close links to the British National Front and other right-wing race-hate thugs.

During the day, all three boys went to Ballysillan primary school. At night, at home in Benview, neo-Nazis crudely painted their windows and doors with swastikas. Some of the extremists couldn't even differentiate between the races they deemed to hate: they called the Shoukris 'Pakis'. Indeed, I once remember mentioning the Shoukris in a phone call to Johnny Adair's estranged wife, Gina. She was still living with 'Mad Dog' in Bolton, England, at the time. 'Them Paki bastards' was her instant and derogatory response, before handing the phone to her then husband.

To their credit—and it may be the only credit you can give them—the Shoukris didn't buckle under the racist bigotry.

According to sources who knew them in Benview, the racism 'gave them skins as thick as a charging rhinoceros, with attitudes to match.'

One acquaintance of the time recalls: 'The three brothers were always up to scheming and working out ways to make a fast buck. They'd have been as much at home in the mean streets of the Bronx as they were in Ballysillan. From an early age they gambled and played in card schools with men much older than themselves.' That probably sowed the seeds of Andre Shoukri, at least, becoming a gambling addict.

The trio became notorious in the teenage gangland 'turf' of the Ballysillan and Westland housing estates, at the upper end of North Belfast, nestling in the shadow of Cave Hill. 'As they grew up,' said a source who was later to be in the ranks of the UDA with them, 'they began to reciprocate the bullying they'd suffered as young boys on others. They saw it as their turn to bully and make a mockery of people. I believe this was a reaction to the way they were bullied as young boys in Benview,' the authoritative source said.

With adolescence, came trouble with the cops. They became joyriders, or 'death' riders as such car thieves are now known in Belfast and elsewhere because of the number of fatalities their uncaring and selfish actions have caused. The Shoukri family moved into the Protestant Westland estate, later to become their main power base when they took over the leadership of North Belfast UDA.

A huge recreation area flanks the estate. Known as the Belfast Waterworks, it embraces a huge pond, an even bigger reservoir, with a river running through it and stretches from the estate down to the Antrim Road, with the Catholic New Lodge Road area skirting its bottom rim.

Once integral to the city's water supplies, it was later converted to a huge park intended for the enjoyment of the public. But it was in this public park that the Shoukris became pests, frequently instigating mob scraps and even riots with what they called 'the Fenians' from the New Lodge Road. 'The Westland estate was generally quiet until they moved in. But they soon began making a nuisance of themselves, much to the disappointment of their mother,' a long-time resident of the Westland, before the Shoukris made it the 'Badlands', told me.

Because of their street fighting, they were sculpting out a reputation for themselves as, in Belfast parlance, 'hard men', but they weren't going into fights alone. The brothers were backing each other up. And their mini-gang of three was often swollen by other teenage hoods who began to hover round and hang on to them.

Like so many other terrorist gangs in Ulster—be they IRA, UDA, UVF or other organisations—loyalties here were not being built to patriotism or political ideology, but to the street: in the school playground or on the pavements of the streets where these young hoods lived. And often the gelling together of the teenage gangs was to metamorphose into terrorism, and then gangsterism and crime.

It was crime that first brought Andre Shoukri into the sights—literally—of the local UDA. Shoukri had 'graduated' from street skullduggery into housebreaking and burglary. He was robbing homes. But more pertinently for the UDA, he was also thieving from businesses and filling stations in North Belfast.

Now, many of these businesses and filling stations were paying money to the UDA for 'protection'. And when their proprietors went running to the local commanders complaining about Andre Shoukri, the UDA bosses had to act. They called Andre in and accused him of 'anti-social behaviour', as was their wont at the time.

And they told him they would either 'cure' him of his petty crime, or cripple him. In other words, he could join their ranks, or he could take a beating, most probably with baseball bats, breaking his arms, or legs, or both. 'Within seconds of the stark choice being put to him, Andre Shoukri chose the first option,' a UDA insider at the time recalled.

Six weeks into his membership, in June 1996, Andre Shoukri was to make his first foray into the media spotlight and into the dock of a court. He was charged with the manslaughter of a promising young tennis player, twenty-three-year-old Gareth Parker from Dublin.

Shoukri and his friends had been drinking in a north-Belfast bar in the aftermath of a controversial annual band parade—the Tour of the North. The parade has, in the past, sparked sectarian violence in the area. Shoukri assaulted Mr Parker who was waiting for a taxi just outside the bar. The Dubliner fell into the road where he was struck and killed by a passing car. In court Shoukri admitted striking the young tennis star. He was convicted of malicious wounding and handed down a two-year sentence. Having served time on remand, he was out in eight months.

When Andre Shoukri went to jail, within a couple of weeks, Ihab Shoukri took his place in the UDA—just as, years later, he was to cover for his younger brother as Brigadier for North Belfast when Andre went back behind bars on a blackmail and extortion rap. By this time, Ihab was starting to build what ballooned into the brothers' drugs empire.

But as the three Shoukris, including the youngest brother, Yuk, grew up, it was recognised, both within the home and without, that Ihab himself was no 'balloon' in the brains sense. 'From early on, it was recognised that he was the one with the smarts, before dealing in drugs, and then becoming hooked on them himself, did his head in,' said a former school pal.

Ironically, for his first four years after primary school, Ihab, alone among the three brothers, was educated in one of Northern Ireland's few integrated schools, Hazlewood College, where Catholics and Protestants are taught side by side. Integrated education had been promoted in Northern Ireland by a former grammar school boy from Belfast, Brian Mawhinney, who had later moved to England and become a member of Margaret Thatcher's Conservative Party.

Most schools in Northern Ireland were, and still are, either State-run (open to all), or Maintained (Catholic, overseen by Catholic Church). The reality is that with Catholic schools catering for children of that tradition, state schools attracted mainly, and in some areas exclusively, Protestants. This meant that, moving through primary and secondary education, most Catholic and Protestant kids never got to sit with each other in class until they reached further education: college or university. But the vast majority, especially if they lived in working-class areas—or 'the ghettoes'—never got that far in the education process, so a new movement sprung up, campaigning for Catholic and Protestant children, and indeed kids from all ethnic and religious backgrounds, regardless of class or creed, to be educated together. As Brian Mawhinney, who had become a 'Direct Rule' minister at Stormont, funnelled special funding out of his education budget into integrated schools they began springing up around Ulster, both in urban and rural areas. And Ihab Shoukri, brought up in tough Protestant working-class areas, was to attend one of the first such schools.

Kudos must be given to his mother, Katie, in sending her eldest son to an integrated secondary school, but again, Katie's well-meant plan was to end in 'disappointment'. Aping his antics on the streets, his behaviour at the College was described as 'erratic' at best. Bullying—him bullying others this time—became a problem, according to one ex-teacher.

For his last year of secondary education, Ihab was moved to the Boys' Model school on the Ballysillan Road, close to the Westland estate. His other two brothers were already there. Now this school has a deservedly sound reputation, renowned for its academic and sporting prowess and for instilling a rigid regime of discipline. I have personal experience of this. I helped coach the Model 1st xv rugby team for a season at the invitation of a friend who taught at the school. They were all a sound bunch of lads. Indeed, one of them, who went on to represent Ireland at Schools level, was a nephew of the former RUC and PSNI Chief Constable, Sir Ronnie Flanagan. This lad came from the Westland estate himself. And he went on to become a policeman—just like his Uncle Ronnie.

A sizeable quota of that 1st xv squad also ended up in police ranks, but Ihab and Andre Shoukri, anything but Model boys, ended up in the ranks of the UDA.

Just before his first major brush with the law—and spell behind bars—Andre had become a bit of a poser in every sense. A local modelling agency, ironically called Pharaohs—another reason for the soubriquet 'The Mummy's Boys'—had him on its books for a short time. Shoukri, as was later to become clear, did not shy away from the camera. Like Adair and Gray before him, he lapped up media attention.

Both brothers shared an old acquaintance who went to the same school, John 'Bonzer' Boreland. Both Andre and Boreland played soccer at the Boys' Model school. Indeed, a brochure of the school's young soccer players, produced for an outing to the 1990 World Cup, carries a picture of Andre Shoukri, aged fourteen.

Of course, the school was not to know then what social and criminal ogres the Shoukris, aided and abetted by 'Bonzer' Boreland, would turn into. There are many boys in that photograph who have since become a credit to the school and leading members of society, both in the business and social senses. But Andre Shoukri, once out from behind bars for his part in Gareth Parker's death, embarked on a distinctly anti-social 'career' from then on.

Not having learned his lesson from being jailed for his part in the death of young Parker, Shoukri and 'Bonzer' Boreland attempted a crude blackmailing scam. They tried to extort money from North Belfast man Mel Lundy, who owned a pizza business. Brave Mr Lundy tipped off the cops, who set up an undercover sting operation. Shoukri and Boreland were caught in the act.

The police convinced Mr Lundy to give evidence against the pair. However, just days after the brazen blackmail duo were convicted and put behind bars, Mel Lundy and his family had to flee Northern Ireland after they were warned of a UDA plot to kill them.

Both wannabe blackmailers were released in 2002, but by this stage, Johnny 'Mad Dog' Adair had pencilled Andre Shoukri in as a possible successor, having met him in prison. Andre was housed in the same UDA wing as 'Mad Dog'. Said one ex-inmate of the time: 'Adair, of course, with his Mr Universe physique, liked to swagger. But Shoukri was also pumping iron before going into jail. He had the same kind of swagger, exuded the same kind of ultra-confidence and bravado.

'He quickly came to 'Mad Dog's' attention. But instead of seeing him as a rival, Adair took a shine to him. He fancied him as an ally, rather than a foe. And both got on. Especially as Adair came to appreciate the hunger Andre had for money, that he was driven by the lust for cash, just like himself.

'Adair saw the money-making potential of Shoukri and himself working in tandem within the UDA—Adair in the West of the city on the Shankill, and Shoukri in the North in the Westland and in Tiger's Bay.'

But the former prisoner also noted that both Adair and Shoukri shared another common interest: 'a love of themselves'. Said the UDA man, a 'lifer' at the time: 'They shared that love of themselves and bodybuilding was to forge a strong bond between this former neo-Nazi Adair and what he would normally have considered as a "black" man.'

The same source also confirmed that Adair and Shoukri shared something else in the prison gym: anabolic steroids, beloved of rogue bodybuilders. 'They weren't only pumping iron in that gym,' he revealed, adding, 'They commandeered all the supplies of steroids being smuggled into the loyalist wings of the jail. It became a competition to see who could pump themselves up to be the biggest physically.'

But both Adair and Shoukri knew that steroids could do them long-term damage. Not just to their livers, as had been proved in the world of sport, where bodybuilders, shot putters and discus throwers had suffered severe side effects. (Indeed, vicious and violent mood swings were later to contribute to the break-up of 'Mad Dog's' marriage to wife Gina. C Company sources on the Shankill charged that it wasn't just because 'Mr Muscles' Adair had become lousy in bed because steroids shrunk his penis. He had also started beating her up.)

Shoukri, the 'incredible bulk', who prided himself on bedding women, didn't want a shrivelled penis, or a shrunken and sick liver, so he switched to a non-prescription painkiller called Nubain. This drug kills the pain of heavy weightlifting. Ihab started bulking up, too, and doing the same. Said a source close to them when both ran the North Belfast Brigade: 'Nubain is closely linked to heroin: as well as the physical effect, it has a similar effect as heroin on the mind. Andre and Ihab became addicted to it. And it's an addiction they still have to this day.'

It was all a long, long way from the early picture published in this book, which shows a dashing, but skinny, Andre Shoukri as a teenager, in white tuxedo and bow tie at a school formal. But even then, he looked like a hitman in the hit TV gangster series *The Sopranos*.

And to the UDA Godfathers this fresh-faced young man would have seemed exactly in tune with the leadership when he made his move to take over from the disgraced Jimbo Simpson as North Belfast UDA boss. Indeed, Adair was to back him then—thanks to that friendship forged behind bars in the now-defunct Maze Prison.

But the Protestant paramilitary, who once looked like he'd walked off the set of *The Sopranos*, would later hit a bum note with the rest of the ruling UDA Inner Council: just like his cell- and soul mate, Johnny 'Mad Dog' Adair.

07 | THE UNTOUCHABLES

The followers of Johnny Adair used to defend him with the mawkish slogan that, 'His Only Crime was Loyalty'. It was the satirical commentator Newton Emerson who turned that line on its head, to read: 'His Only Loyalty Was Crime'. And it was the *Sunday World* that began to hammer that message home.

But if 'His Only Loyalty Was Crime' summed up 'Mad Dog', the Shoukri brothers, Andre and Ihab, were that grandiose and greedy maxim—plus two.

But not at the time they took over the reigns of power of the North Belfast UDA—just one of the six Brigades which formed, don't forget, the biggest paramilitary organisation in Northern Ireland, Catholic or Protestant. Then, they simply assumed the joint mantle of Johnny 'Mad Dog' Adair and Jim 'Doris Day' Gray.

They became copycat 'Brigadiers of Bling'. They both hit the gym. They ballooned. They became caricatures of Mr Universe contestants. They were no longer shooting steroids into their veins like Adair and his mob on the Shankill to 'bulk up' into mini-Arnold Schwarzeneggers, but they were taking other drugs that had the same effect.

Almost immediately, they started living the gangster lifestyle so ostentatiously it was obscene, off their own, Protestant, working-class people. The UDA, way at the start of the Troubles when it was first set up on Belfast's Woodvale Road as the WDA (Woodvale Defence Association) had vowed to protect its community from republican attacks as a kind of street-patrolling, vigilante organisation. Now, it proved a hollow pledge. The Shoukris were into protection, all right. But it was protection rackets and extortion they were into: fleecing their own community, prostituting their own people.

Building contractors constructing homes for people in north Belfast were threatened that if they didn't pay protection money, their workers—and especially Catholic workers— would be shot dead. They were told the UDA knew where their children went to school, where their wives shopped. The threat of the kidnapping of their loved ones—or worse, their murder—loomed large in the lives of such contractors. The result? Some of them paid up. Others simply pulled out of the site, pulled their workers off the job. And one consequence was that work stopped on housing projects in Protestant areas. People who needed roofs over their heads didn't get them.

Why? Because of the Shoukris.

The gang also milked local shopkeepers, builders, bar-owners, and at one stage even tried to hijack a downtown Belfast nightclub. And, of course, they were to poison the areas in which their brigade operated with drugs, just like Adair and Gray had done to their 'turfs' before them.

The Shoukris ran their drugs empire from a bar on a main road in Belfast, close to Tiger's Bay down at the docks. The pub was called The Alexandra. A good man had owned that pub, but like many other businesses in Ulster, when the paramilitaries muscle in, there is little the proprietor can do. Try to 'bar' them, or tell them their kind isn't wanted, and your pub, probably the result of a lifetime's graft (most Irish pubs are owned by people who started as barmen, and worked their way up to owning their own premises) can end in a pile of ashes. Torched. And you are lucky if you aren't part of the pyre.

Incredibly, The Alexandra, on Belfast's York Road, was just 500 metres from a police barracks on the other side of the road, but it was in that bar that, at weekends in particular, the Shoukris were to entice young people from throughout north Belfast to deal drugs for them.

The lure of easy money from drugs attracted others from unlikely backgrounds to join the Shoukris and their gang in peddling drugs and poisoning youngsters. One was an ex-prison officer, of all people. He had been discharged out of the prison service as disabled, but, even confined to a wheelchair, he worked the door on weekend nights charging a 'cover price' into raves in the back of the pub, and also charging the kids for their Ecstasy and their 'blow'—cannabis—to make joints.

But the Shoukris had one major fault. Both Andre and Ihab shared it. In short, they thought they were The Untouchables. They believed, for a long time, that they were beyond the long arm of the law. Their sheer arrogance in how they strutted about and conducted their 'business'—especially Andre, bedecked in his bling (thick gold chain round neck and wrist, designer watch, designer clothes), swanning around working-class areas in his 'Beamer', his brand new emerald green BMW—underpinned their 'untouchable' status.

But cracks were beginning to appear. Andre's gambling, punting almost a million pounds in a year on the horses, got up the noses of ordinary working-class men who were in the 'cream cookies', the bookies, and could only afford to punt a few quid—a tenner at the most—on the horses. Many of them were veteran UDA members. Many of them wondered where Andre Shoukri was getting the money to gamble Las Vegas-style.

UDA bosses began to wonder, too.

Discreetly, Irish President Mary McAleese's husband, Martin, a Dublin businessman, had got a few of his business friends to round-robin into a fund aimed at helping kids in the loyalist Westland estate in North Belfast: which, of course, was also the Shoukris' paramilitary base at the time. President McAleese's spouse and his business acquaintances stumped up around £20,000 which was supposed to help establish a sports initiative for youngsters in the housing complex. The cash came north of the border from the philanthropists who teamed up with well-meaning Martin McAleese. Andre Shoukri blatantly put his sticky fingers in that particular till and stole £17,000 of the money meant for the kids.

It, too, went over the bookies' counter.

But still, the UDA hierarchy stood by him. The organisation's 'main man', Jackie McDonald, before he fell out with Shoukri, even staged a Press conference with a rival newspaper to the *Sunday World*, the *Sunday Life,* to allow Andre Shoukri to deny his gambling habit. McDonald sat side-by-side with Shoukri in the UDA's main office in Sandy Row in the south of the city and allowed Shoukri to slag off his *Sunday World* pseudonym of 'The Bookies' Brigadier', and to deny, point blank, that he was punting thousands of pounds every day.

When I hit back at the story in the *World* the following week, graffiti went up, painted boldly in capital letters at a busy traffic junction at the corner of Sandy Row: 'JIM McDOWELL READS THE SUNDAY LIFE'.

That went up on a Saturday night. I was away filming that weekend, working on a series for the BBC. I was presenting a film about the border, the main theme of which was that this

contentious frontier, which had caused so much trouble in
Ireland down all the years, had now virtually disappeared. I
had just finished a piece to camera saying of the Border: 'You
can't see it, you can't feel it, you can't touch it...' when I got a
call on my mobile. The voice on the other end said, 'McDowell,
you should see the graffiti that's gone up on the corner of
Sandy Row!'

My contact told me what it was. I must admit, I had to laugh.
Everybody—especially in UDA ranks—knew who I worked for.
A virtual billboard-size plug for the *Sunday World*, and for *free!*

But Jackie McDonald, and Andre Shoukri, didn't have much to
laugh about the following Sunday. Because it was then we published yet another story. This revealed that not only had Jackie
McDonald sat with Andre Shoukri in an act of solidarity as
Shoukri lied about his gambling addiction, but then, according
to our sources inside the North Belfast UDA, Shoukri walked
straight out of that staged press conference in Sandy Row, drove
back into north Belfast, walked into his regular bookies—and
planked another ten grand on a horse.

When we ran that story, it wiped the smile off a few UDA
faces, and at the top level, too. For 'The Bookies' Brigadier' had
not only made a fool of himself. He'd made a mug of the UDA
and its leader, Jackie McDonald himself. Plus, it was becoming
clear—even to the UDA—that Shoukri was mugging their
coffers to pay for his increasing gambling debts, now spiralling
close to a million quid. He was 'fingered', again within UDA
ranks, when £10,000 of European-Union funding for a loyalist
ex-prisoners' project on his turf mysteriously disappeared:
further funding was frozen. And then there was the farce over
the 'Big Fight Night' Andre Shoukri was supposed to take part
in, to raise money for cancer charities. He trousered ten grand
raised in ticket sales for that, as will be revealed. Then there was

his abortive bid to annex the ownership of the Network night-club in Belfast.

The 'Bookies' Brigadier' was becoming desperate. Hooked on betting, a big-time loser on the gee-gees who, because of his gambling addiction, always thought the next bet would be the 'big' one, he needed to recoup the money he'd stolen from UDA coffers. He ordered his closest cohorts out on ill-planned and equally ill-fated bank robberies and Tiger kidnap attempts. As a result, in the space of just one year—between 2005 and 2006—more than twenty-five North Belfast UDA men ended up behind bars because of Andre Shoukri's seemingly insatiable quest for more and more money.

The Inner Council became suspicious. One senior source there told me at the start of 2006: 'He is either sacrificing his own men—or he is setting them up to be lifted by police because they know too much. He's sending them out on "operations"—and then touting on them.' Other veterans within the ranks of the North Belfast Brigade harboured similar suspicions.

And then, according to our sources, Jackie McDonald was tipped off about the 'sticky fingers in the till' embezzlement of the money sent up North from Martin McAleese and his busi-ness friends. According to one insider, that caused 'acute embarrassment' to McDonald because of his closeness to President McAleese and her well-meaning husband Martin.

You'd think that Shoukri and his swindling sidekick John 'Bonzer' Boreland would have learned from their previous abortive blackmailing of Mel Lundy when both ended up behind bars, but not a bit of it. Here, again, it was to be a case of *déjà vu*—or, what kind of DummiesRU?

Just as in the Lundy case, Shoukri and 'Bonzer' decided they'd put the boot in for blackmail. This time, they targeted a bar. At first, the manageress and her partner complied. But the demands from the mobsters kept increasing, until they could take no more, so just like Mel Lundy before them, they decided to co-operate in a 'sting' operation. The blackmailers were bugged. And, just like in the Lundy case, the bungling blackmailers ended up behind bars.

Here's what happened. This woman—who to this day can only be named as 'Witness A'—was running a bar, which also cannot be named, in North Belfast, smack dab in the 'turf' which 'Brigadier' Shoukri thought he controlled, and where he thought he was indeed untouchable.

Why can 'Witness A', in her mid-thirties, and the bar, not be named? Because a Judge said so. The same also goes for 'Witness B' in the case, who is in his forties, and was 'Witness A's' partner. But both agreed to work with anti-terror detectives to put Shoukri and the two others in his blackmailing mob behind bars.

Even before the court case started, Witnesses A and B had to be whisked out of Northern Ireland and kept under armed police guard, in protective custody at a secret address. But before Andre Shoukri, John 'Bonzer' Boreland, and a third wannabe blackmailer, Terry Harbinson, eventually copped their pleas, Judge Mr Justice Hart put down a blanket ban on reporting their identities at a special hearing in Belfast's Crown Court.

The prosecution had filed an application for reporting restrictions to be placed on Witnesses A, B and C. Judge Hart granted it when he starkly ordered: 'By virtue of Section 46(6) of the Youth Justice and Criminal Evidence Act 1999, it is ordered that no matter relating to the persons referred to in this proceedings as Witness A, Witness B or Witness C shall, during the lifetime of that person, be included in any publication if it is likely to lead members of the public to identify that person as being a witness to the proceedings.'

The ruling that no details of the witnesses can be published 'in any publication' during their lifetime applied to the *Sunday World*. We know who they are. But we couldn't, and can't name them. Not just because the Judge ordered it. But because we believe they are very brave and courageous people.

So why did they do it? Because they were driven close to bankruptcy, were at their wits' end, and, like many of the victims of the Shoukri mob's extortion rackets before them, they feared for their lives—and that of their families.

Here's the timetable which saw the bungling blackmail trio of terror put back behind bars.

June 2004:
Witness A takes over the north Belfast bar, ironically once a favourite pub of the teachers from Shoukri and Boreland's old school. The teachers like dropping in there for a bite of lunch, or a pint after school, or to celebrate special occasions.

Shoukri and Boreland demand £1,000 a week from Witness A. She is acutely aware that both are UDA 'heavies'. She bargains them down, but is forced, against her will, to pay them £200 a week—which at that stage would have totalled £10,400 a year…or the equivalent of selling over 4,000 pints of beer before she even opened her doors!

June–November 2004
The protection money is paid on a regular basis. But Shoukri and Boreland start treating the pub like their own. They order drink without paying—often for gangs of their henchmen, they lift carry-outs without paying, often expensive bottles of vodka, whiskey and spirits, effectively stealing the liquor. They even help themselves to the cash in the gaming machines.

Witness A and her partner Witness B are getting to breaking point. They are aware that a previous owner of the pub, who tried to stand up to Shoukri's mob, got a terrible beating, and later sold the premises. But more pressure was to be applied to Witness A and her partner.

December 2004:
Boreland books a wedding reception—not his own—to be held at the bar, paying £500 to put on the food at the wedding bash. But once it's over, he demands the money back. He says that since he brought business to the bar—he alleges that lots of money was spent on drink by the guests—he should not have to cover the food. He also asks for another 2,000 quid, as his 'cut' of the 'takings' at the wedding reception. He is told that the wedding party brought in nothing like that. But he gets the original 500 quid he asked for, plus another grand on top of that.

January–May 2005:
Shoukri and his gangsters turn the screw even more. They're milking the bar of more and more money. The court would hear that by the spring of that year, 'the amount of money being taken meant no profit was being made'. By the end of May, the business is going to the wall, and Witness A and her partner are forced to launch, literally, a Mayday sos—to their families and friends. They borrow £4,000 from them, just to keep Boreland and Co. off their backs.

But 'Bonzer' wants to break the bank. He and Harbinson confront Witness B. A gun is put to his head. He is forced to hand over the books and keys to the bar. With their spirits—never mind the bank—almost broken, the pub partners decide on a last, drastic action. They know the risks involved. They know they are going to have to live their lives in secret for a long time—possibly a lifetime—under the shadow of the gunman. But they go to the police.

July 2005:

Cops launch an undercover operation. It 'involved the covert recording of conversations', as the court would later hear. We reported it more tabloid-style at the time. We said the bar was bugged. And Shoukri, Boreland and Harbinson are mugged—by the very folk they fleeced, cruelly and illegally, for the previous year.

The terror trio are arrested. Charged under his full name of Andre Khaled Shoukri, and twenty-eight at the time, he is accused of eighteen crimes, including blackmail, intimidation and acquiring criminal property.

John 'Bonzer' Boreland, from Sunningdale Gardens in North Belfast, ten years older than Shoukri, is charged with four counts of blackmail, one of intimidation, and one of possessing a firearm, or imitation firearm, to commit assault. Terry Harbinson, then twenty-five, is accused of blackmail, intimidation and possession.

November, 2007:

Crunchtime in the courtroom. The Press grapevine has been abuzz for months with speculation that Shoukri and his two blackmailing compadres are going to cop a plea. Why? Because it might be exposed during a trial that at least one of them—and internal UDA sources are already pointing the finger at Andre Shoukri—is a police tout and has been for years.

So on Friday, 30 November 2007, Shoukri, Boreland and Harbinson all appeared at Belfast Crown Court in front of Judge Mr Justice Treacy. And after spending a fortune in tax-payers' money—they were all on legal aid for the two years they spent behind bars on remand—on defence applications to various courts and other ploys which finally proved fruitless in the face of the law, the terror trio did, indeed, cop pleas. That

Friday, they all entered guilty pleas to an extensive catalogue of almost thirty crimes.

Shoukri and Boreland were sentenced to nine years each, Harbinson to seven years. Jailing Shoukri, the Judge reminded him that he'd also been guilty of a double whammy by attempting a blackmail scam for the second time. Justice Mr Treacy told him that apart from his 'belated' pleas of guilty, 'there was little that could be said on your behalf by way of mitigation given the grave nature of the offences and the fact that you have a previous conviction for blackmail, also involving commercial premises in the same area as the present offences.' That was a clear reference to the earlier Mel Lundy case.

Standing in the dock, it should have embarrassed Shoukri. But the smirk on his face belied that... Shoukri already knew that as he and Boreland had already served two years in Maghaberry jail on remand, with fifty per cent remission, they could be back on the streets of Belfast by 2010—if the UDA let them, that is.

But as he was being led back down to the holding cell under Belfast's Laganside Court, if Shoukri had been able to hear what the top cop whose team put him away was saying outside, it would have wiped that smirk clean off his coupon. Talking to reporters, PSNI Detective Inspector Mark Brown also used the word 'untouchable'. 'They thought they were above the law. You could say they thought they were untouchable.'

He said that what both the cops and courts had combined to do was 'a clear demonstration that individuals who commit serious crime will be pursued by the police and, when convicted, go to prison for a long time.'

DI Brown said one other thing which had particular resonance at this time. He said that the jailing of Andre Shoukri, Boreland and Harbinson 'has had the effect of dismantling the leadership of the UDA in North Belfast.'

The senior policeman was only partially right. Because the UDA leadership were on a twin track on that one. They had already started the process of 'dismantling' the leadership of the self-deluded 'Untouchables', too. And it had kicked off against Andre and Ihab even before Andre copped his plea and was sentenced to nine years in pokey.

The run-up to Andre Shoukri's trial was to bring us face-to-face for the first, and only, time. And that court hearing brought one of our hairiest moments—or, rather, thirty-five minutes—with the Shoukri mob.

As he was in the dock in the Crown Court at Laganside for a remand hearing, I was sitting on the Press benches. We'd heard Shoukri was to be in court on the Saturday morning after he'd been lifted. Hugh Jordan and I decided to go. It would make the splash, the Page 1 story, for the next day.

We knew that a team of 'heavies' would attend the hearing, too, to show their (then) 'solidarity' with Shoukri. But we thought, What the hell, there'll be plenty of police there to look after us if they start on us. In the event, police reinforcements had to be summoned to the court—by us!

As soon as we walked to the second floor of the court—a mezzanine floor with a balcony perched forty feet up from the ground—we knew we were in trouble. A thirty-strong mob of UDA thugs haemorrhaged into the wide corridor between the courtroom doors and the balcony.

As soon as they spotted Hugh and me, the growlers started. Insults flew. One of the heavies even came over to me and shoved into me with his shoulder. This was right at the precipice of the balcony. A few months earlier, a protagonist in a bitter court battle had tried to throw someone over that balcony!

Normally, we'd have told these gangsters what to do with themselves. But there were only two cops in that corridor, and there were only two of us. And there were thirty of them, getting more and more threatening.

We decided it was best if we headed into the court. Sometimes, in high-profile paramilitary cases like this, the courtroom itself is lined with riot cops in their baseball caps and jumpsuits, kitted out for any trouble, but there weren't any today. So as the heavies streamed into court and kept growling and glaring at me from the public gallery, Hugh nipped into the alcove between the court doors.

Musgrave Street police station sits just round the corner from the Laganside courts. It would only take the cops a couple of minutes to get from there to the courts. Hugh phoned Musgrave Street on his mobile, and asked for the duty sergeant. And within minutes a squad of police—fronted up by a sergeant we knew from the rugby—was both inside and outside the courtroom.

But even at that, when Shoukri himself came into the dock— to be greeted by the usual clarion call of welcome and clenched-fist salutes from the gougers in the public gallery— he simply stared straight across the courtroom: at me. And he hardly took his eyes off me the whole time of the short hearing, before he was remanded in custody and taken back to the cells.

Now, some people may have been unnerved by that. And I'm no hero. As I've said many times, any man who says he doesn't feel fear—ever—is a fool—but I wasn't afraid. Instead, I took Shoukri's steely and simmering stare as a compliment. We had done our jobs, again. We had helped get Andre Shoukri where we had always argued he belonged. Behind bars.

08 | THE CHOCOLATE SOLDIERS

Andre Shoukri was used to ordering his 'heavies' about, but in other UDA circles he, his brother Ihab, and the rest of their crew were known as 'chocolate soldiers'. 'Mad Dog' Adair himself dubbed them that when they fell out with him, as he claimed they'd never been in the front line during the 'bad old days' taking the fight, as he saw it, to the IRA. And don't forget, when Andre Shoukri himself was handed a mission to shoot Adair, he was 'fortuitously' stopped by cops while carrying the gun: and got off, many senior UDA still believe, because he didn't have the b***s to do it.

Still, while out of jail, he believed he had the 'muscle' to order a dog off a butcher's cart, never mind order his 'chocolate' dogs of war about.

It was that kind of arrogance that spurred Shoukri to phone me personally one day, and issue another, albeit veiled, threat. He had got my mobile phone number from somewhere, and the first time he had the temerity to contact me was on a Friday night, when I was out with my wife and some friends in Nick's Warehouse, close to the *Sunday World* office in Belfast.

I got a tip-off that Shoukri and some of his most trusted lieutenants were downtown, cruising about in a car that wasn't
Andre Shoukri's trademark 'Beamer'. I knew the tip-off was
genuine. It came from a top cop I knew and trusted. He didn't
even have to phone me. He was standing beside me, at the bar
in Nick's.

Shoukri and his 'team' had obviously been scouting out a few
pubs in the area of our office that early Friday night. They'd
probably clocked me through the giant plate-glass windows
fronting Nick's. And I'm not that hard to spot. With the baldy
head and my build, I'm something akin to the Donaghadee
lighthouse in County Down, that Brendan Behan was once
sent up to paint by the Irish Lights authority.

Anyway, Shoukri and his crew had obviously tippled to
where I was having an after-work tipple. So he calls me, and
tells me he knows where I am. He says he's 'in the area', and he
would like to speak to me, 'personally. Just for about twenty
minutes,' he says. 'It won't take any longer than that. I just want
a wee talk with you,' he says.

Now, I'm no Toby Jug—no mug. I tell Shoukri what to do
with his 'invite', and with himself. I cut off the phone call. I tell
my friends in the bar what has happened, especially the policeman who wired me off in the first place. He's interested. Very
interested.

He tells me, of course, what I already know. 'Don't go anywhere near that bastard. The twenty minutes he's offering to
meet you for will be the last twenty minutes of your life.'

But as he's talking to me, the off-duty cop is already on the
phone to his colleagues. As he's talking to them, he's talking to
me. 'If that bastard comes back on the phone again—and he
must be on something to even come up with this crazy idea in
the first place—offer him a deal he can't refuse. Tell him to
come and meet you. In here. And I'll have a few boys waiting.'

Incredibly, and again underlining 'The Untouchables' syndrome, Shoukri rang me back.

'Look,' he said, 'I mean you no harm. I just want a yarn. Nothing will happen to you.'

Yeah... and the Pope's a Free Presbyterian.

So I tell him I'll meet him, not in a car, as he is punting, but in public. Either inside or outside where I'm standing having a pint, in big Nick Price's place. And I tell him I'll meet him on my own, just the two of us.

He's dithering. But others in the scout car with him are muttering in the background. I hear one of them say: 'It could be a set-up...'

And how right he was. Because as I was talking to Shoukri on my mobile, the cop was talking to his boys on the other. They weren't too far away, either. They could have been at Nick's in a matter of minutes.

But Shoukri wouldn't bite. He was still trying to persuade me to meet him for 'a friendly yarn': but on his terms, meeting him in that car with his cohorts which, he said, was parked 'not too far away.' I refused. Point blank. (And rightly so. For such an invite into a car was later to cost Johnny Adair's former 'military commander' in C Company, 'Bucky' McCullough, his life: and Shoukri's former buddy on the Shankill Road, William 'Mo' McCourtney, was sentenced to eight years for manslaughter after admitting that killing).

Anyway, after I snubbed Shoukri—for all-too-obvious reasons—he and his 'team' took off back to north Belfast: just minutes before cops, summoned by my policeman friend, hit the street outside Nick's.

So literally, Shoukri and his squad had done a runner—in the Nick's, rather than the nick, of time. But what had sparked this bizarre—and dangerous—invitation to an impromptu parley?

Two *Sunday World* stories, which really got up Shoukri's nose.

One involved his mob's attempt to hijack a downtown Belfast nightclub and turn it into a drugs den. The other was the boxing match, in which Andre Shoukri himself planned to be the main attraction on the fight bill in the notoriously hard district of Tiger's Bay in Belfast.

Along with nearby 'Sailortown', Tiger's Bay and the neighbouring 'Half Bap' district close to Belfast docks, had bred the hardest of men. Among them were legends like 'Buck Alex' Robinson, a 'minder' and renowned bare-knuckle streetfighter who kept two lions—albeit toothless ones—in his backyard, and walked them along York Street, much as the working men of Belfast would walk their greyhounds in the street before taking them to the city's Celtic Park and Dunmore Stadium dog-racing tracks.

Sailortown also spawned Rinty Monaghan, the world flyweight boxing champion, whose reputation was doubly enhanced, as a fleet-footed and -fisted fighter, and as a travelling minstrel whose signature tune, before punches flew in the ring, was 'The Londonderry Air', better known simply as 'Danny Boy.'

Andre Shoukri's delusions of grandeur—and of being a hard man cut out of the same cloth as both 'Buck Alex' and Belfast's own original 'Lord of the Ring' Rinty Monaghan—obviously overcame him. He was into bulking up, albeit with the use of non-prescription drugs. He was pumping iron, too, although when he tried to become a regular user of one gym, they told him he couldn't continue training there, throwing him the line that it was for his own safety. That he'd been spotted going in and out and may be a target for either the IRA—or, indeed, his own enemies within the UDA. It worked. He stopped going there.

Still, he owned a luxury house—and also ran a business—in the Country Antrim town of Ballyclare—and here, he built his own mini-gym. He bulked up. He eventually became a cross between Sylvester Stallone's Rambo and Shrek. And, for some reason, he fancied himself as a fighter. Even 'though the 'oul' hands' in the UDA had dubbed him a 'chocolate soldier', or maybe even because of that, because he thought he had to prove himself as a 'macho man'.

But, bizarrely, he decided he would not only promote his own boxing bill in Tiger's Bay, he would take part in it himself and, what's more, he would be top of the bill!

Now, the word on the street was that the money raised from 'Big Fight Night' would go to a cancer charity. But the word on the street got to me first. We blew the gaffe on the paraCelebs' pugilistic promotion and to be honest, we took the p*** out of it. We openly wondered in print whether the money raised would go to this cancer charity or end up over a bookie's counter, like the Martin McAleese philanthropic funds before it, and much of the UDA's money in between.

Shoukri went nuts. He'd lined up a team of his own lieutenants to take on other opponents in the ring. Many of them were loathe: they were to boxing what Mahatma Ghandi would have been to Mike Tyson. As it was, Shoukri was to take on a Sunday-School teacher, but no novice when it came to the noble art covered by the Queensberry Rules. His name was Michael Madden, and somewhat incredibly for a Christian who preaches the gospel of turning the other cheek, Michael's brother Brian, a local pastor—known from his schooldays as 'Brains'—was fronting up the fisticuffs feast!

In the end, it didn't happen, though. Andre Shoukri may have thought he was next in line behind the fallen 'Brigadiers of Bling' Johnny 'Mad Dog' Adair and Jim 'Doris Day' Gray in the so-called paraCelebs stakes. But there were others who thought differently.

First, the plug was pulled on the original venue, in the heart of Tiger's Bay. Pastor 'Brains' then tried to switch the bizarre boxing show to the Ballysillan Leisure Centre, close to the other Shoukri-Brigade heartland of the Westland estate. But it was owned by Belfast City Council. And given the UDA's reputation, nationalist and republican councillors in City Hall—and to be fair, quite a few unionist and loyalist councillors—were having none of that. They stopped the Ballysillan Leisure Centre bouts going ahead on what could be called in boxing parlance a TKO—a Technical Knock-Out.

And WHO did Shoukri blame for the whole scrapping shambles? Yours truly.

But that wasn't the only thing he blamed me for. In the summer of 2006 a very brave young mother-of-two came to me. Her name is Karen McGoldrick.

She'd been married to a guy called Frank McGoldrick, the father of her two kids. Frank had worked with ex-prisoners before becoming something of an entrepreneur. He took over a nightclub in the centre of Belfast, called the Network, in the city's Lower North Street. McGoldrick had been running the club with the help of Karen, until he met an untimely death, leaving his young widow to run the Network.

The Shoukris thought she was an 'easy touch', so much so, she told me, that even while behind bars in prison at one stage, Andre Shoukri had sent an 'emissary' to her. The 'emissary' told Karen McGoldrick that Shoukri wanted no less than *five hundred quid a week* from her in protection money.

Karen McGoldrick refused. She wasn't going to pay paramilitaries and secondly, she simply couldn't afford to pay it.

So what did Shoukri's mob do? They tried to hijack her club. They used the ex-prison officer in the wheelchair, who was the doorman at The Alexandra Bar, as their front man. He was to run the club. They even tried to vault over Karen McGoldrick's head and had the effrontery, literally, to apply to Belfast City Council for a licence to run her club. The police tippled to what was happening, though, and a senior cop turned up at the Council Committee meeting to scupper the Shoukri club-hijacking plan. He told the shocked committee members tasked with doling out entertainment licences that he believed the club would be run by paramilitaries.

However, that left Karen McGoldrick in limbo. She also needed an entertainments licence to run the club, by now tainted by the 'paramilitaries' tag. And in spite of running a lone, one-woman campaign to be able to open the club again, she failed.

But she was brave in coming to us. She lived in loyalist east Belfast, which compounded her courage in coming forward to *Sunday World* to tell her story.

When we ran the story, we ko'd Shoukri's plans to hijack a nightclub right in the heart of Belfast: and what a coup that would have been for them. And Andre Shoukri had suffered a TKO on his aborted boxing scam. That double blow led to another phone call from him to me which was as sinister as the first. But, because of the circumstances in which it was made, it gave us all in the *Sunday World* a good laugh—and made for a great front page.

09 | THE BUNGLING BRIGADIERS

It was a Thursday lunchtime, before Shoukri was lifted on the pub-extortion rap. I was standing at the bar in the Morning Star having a pint. Nothing serious. No story contact to meet, just standing with a couple of mates chawwing the cud, as they say, in one of the great—but increasingly rare—traditional Belfast boozers.

During the Troubles, the city, not exactly teeming with tourists, lost many of its best bars through bombs. Now, it's bulldozers driven by greed. The traditional pubs, which should be tourist Meccas the way they are in Dublin, are being sold off, in many cases to feed the property boom and build apartments. And that's a great pity: not only for punters like myself, but for the city.

The Morning Star, a great bar in the old tradition, thankfully survives.

I'm the butt of constant banter from my mates because of the frequency with which the mobile phone goes. Of course, it's the bane of every hack. Many a good pint of stout has gone stale because we answer the call of the mobile, either from contacts, from 'the office', or, in our case, two offices, North and South.

But as usual, when it goes off this Thursday, I answer it.

And as I desert my pint at the bar counter with the banter ringing in my cauliflower ears—'Why don't you turn that bloody thing off!' or, 'That's the wife—again!' or, even worse, 'Are you away before buying your round—again?'—a voice says: 'It's Andre.'

As I go out through the skinny, twin swing doors of the Morning Star, I ask, 'Andre who?'

'Andre Shoukri,' comes the reply, and without, missing a beat, a question follows: 'Why are you still writing lies about me?'

Now, I can tell instantly from the timbre of his voice that he's on something. And knowing his record, it's not drink. I was to find out later what it was. But for the moment I tell him, 'We don't tell lies about you, or anyone else. We report the truth, especially about how people like you are prostituting your own communities.'

He goes into a rant. But a measured rant. He goes over the stories I've already mentioned. The aborted boxing bill. The Network nightclub. Other stuff we'd printed about him and his mob.

I counter the lot. But he's insistent, although there is a slight, but distinct, slur to his voice. He's most angry about the boxing. 'That money was going to help charity, to help fight cancer,' he tells me.

I tell him that the word, even in his then-heartland of Tiger's Bay, was that the scraps bill was going to be a scam. And that even his own men suspected that the money was going into his pocket, and then to the bookies round the corner to be punted on the gee-gees. I also tell him that we understand from sources inside the UDA, and even inside his own camp, that he 'bottled' out of the boxing bill because he knows that Michael Madden, even though he was a born-again Christian Sunday-school teacher, is a hard man. And that had Shoukri taken him on, he might not only have lost the fight, but lost a lot of face as well.

That's the only time he gets close to losing the bap (losing the head). And I detect he is playing to an audience with this phone call. That there are others in the background 'earywig-ging' in Belfast street slang, listening in. I'm getting more than a bit brassed off with his banging on about us, so eventually, I say to him: 'By the way, how did you get my mobile number?'

Suddenly, the phone conversation is cut off.

I thought it was at his end, so I go back into the pub. My pint of stout has gone stale. To get a fresh one, I have to buy a round, much to the amusement of my mates. So Shoukri achieved one thing with his out-of-the-blue phone call: a few quid to set the pints up—for the second time that lunchtime.

I'm back at the bar talking rugby with Malone RFC men: Malone RFC is the working-class east-Belfast club known collo-quially as 'The Cregagh Road Red Sox'. And my mobile goes again. The lads are going berserk. 'For God's sake McDowell, drop that thing into your pint, instead of drinking it'. That sort of thing.

As it turns out, it's a text message.

Now, some other people are dyslexic. I'm dystextic. I had to ask one of them to get me into the text message. It was Shoukri. I'd already told the boys in the pub about his phone call. They didn't believe me. When the boys saw the text message, they believed me this time...

In the text message, Shoukri actually accused me of cutting *him* off during the previous call. But three things about the text message were eye-openers. First, the spelling was appalling, even given it was a text message. Second, he said I should apologise for cutting him off: even though I didn't. He claimed I was 'disrespecting' him. And third, by texting me, he'd inadvertently given *me* his mobile phone number: something I'd been trying, in vain, to get for months!

That was the funny bit. But there's more, as a famous Ulster comedian used to say. I wrote Shoukri's mobile number down on a beer mat and went back outside again into the entry, and I phoned him straight back.

'Yes?' came the reply.

'McDowell here. I didn't cut off our phone conversation. I thought you did. And I'm apologising for nothing.'

There was, as they say, a pregnant, even startled, pause. 'Where did you get my mobile number?' Shoukri asked.

I had to smile as I replied: 'From your text message, Andre. It was on the text message you just sent me.'

And while he absorbed the fact that he himself had just blown his number cover to me, and voluntarily at that, my next salvo was: 'By the way, Andre, you do know you're not supposed to be talking to the *Sunday World*. None of you are. Big Jackie (McDonald) has put the word out. I don't think he and the rest of the Inner Council will be too pleased at you talking to me.'

At the time of this strange communication, there was another UDA fatwah against the *Sunday World*. An edict had gone out from the top ordering that, because of increasing 'insider' leaks to us, no one, and in particular no one of brigadier rank, was to talk to us.

'You're not even supposed to be reading the *Sunday World*,' I continued. 'Yet you're able to tell me what we're writing about you.'

Shoukri spluttered that he hadn't read the paper himself. 'Somebody' had told him what we were writing about him. In great detail obviously.

In the background, I overheard a female voice, close to Shoukri telling him: 'Put that phone down. Stop talking to him.' The phone went dead. For a second time. And, again, it wasn't me who ended the call. Why should I? I was beginning to enjoy it…

And when I went back to work and told the folk there what had happened, they were amazed, amused and delighted. After all, it was still only Thursday lunchtime. But now we had got our front-page splash for the weekend, courtesy of Andre Shoukri. As North Belfast Brigadier, he had just given us an exclusive interview, in spite of the UDA hierarchy putting a gag on every member of the organisation!

That caused some ructions in the ranks when the paper appeared the following Sunday. Because not only did we run the phone conversations—and text—verbatim. We billed it as an 'EXCLUSIVE INTERVIEW' with a UDA Brigadier… who was behind the organisation's latest boycott of us, and we splashed with the story—on the front page…

10 | THE REAL THING

When Andre was first jailed on remand on the bar blackmail charges in 2006, he tried to hang on to the reins of power from prison, but he was finding it impossible to be a paraMafia Godfather in exile. And he knew the Inner Council were moving to put him into permanent exile from UDA ranks—just like they had with 'Mad Dog' Adair and 'Doris Day' Gray, the brigadier Andre himself had refused to vote out of the organisation. So, while still on remand, he ceded his title of North Belfast Brigadier to his older brother, Ihab.

But the bosses in the mainstream UDA didn't fancy that. They'd had enough of the three previous 'Brigadiers of Bling'—Adair, Gray and Andre Shoukri. They weren't going to wear, literally, another: Ihab. In any case, they had another candidate for North Belfast Brigadier waiting in the wings, in the shape of John Bunting. Also from the Westland housing estate off Belfast's Cave Hill Road, he was a UDA veteran who supported the move away from 'militarism' into community activism and politics. He was earning his spurs—under the 'tutelage' of the late Sammy Duddy—helping to shape, get recognition of, and respect for, the UDA's emerging political arm, the Ulster Political Research Group (UPRG).

He was, in brief, one of Jackie McDonald's 'boys': a trusted aide to the top man. He, too, believed that Andre, Boreland, Ihab and the rump of the Shoukri mob should be removed from UDA ranks, but there were problems. Tensions were running telegraph-pole high at the time: at one meeting, way 'out of the road', in Bushmills, County Antrim, a hard core of the mainstream supposedly gathered in secret session to 'discuss the future' of the leadership of the North Belfast Brigade.

Ihab's mob found out. They lived up to their name. They mobbed the meeting. Similarly, another 'council of war' being held in a north Belfast pub lived up, or down, to its name: it ended in just that — a bust-in followed by a bust-up.

And there was another complication. The South-East Antrim (SEA) Brigade of the UDA, spearheaded by Brigadier Gary Fisher and his one-time UPRG consigliere, Tommy 'Millions' Kirkham, were refusing to back any move on the Shoukris. They had dealt with them in drugs and other crimes, something the *Sunday World* had ruthlessly and relentlessly exposed. They were maintaining a 'neutral' position as a mainstream UDA coup against the Shoukris and their mob loomed. In fact, they were adopting exactly the same stance Andre Shoukri had adopted in the crunch vote over the sacking of Jim Gray. We dubbed them the 'rebel' and 'breakaway' Brigade. The mainstream were later to expel them, too. That split is reported later in the book.

But sacking the Shoukris—the duo who thought themselves 'untouchable', according to the top cop who put away Andre— came first on the Inner Council's agenda. McDonald 'loyalists' like Bunting and Duddy had been busy compiling a secret dossier of the Shoukri regime's 'crimes'. They had also built a base of North Belfast UDA men, many of them veterans, who wanted the Shoukris shafted, too.

In June 2006, while Andre was still on remand, we ran a Page-1 headline that the UDA were to sack the Shoukris. Two days later, on the Tuesday, the Inner Council did just that. Said a source close to the Inner Council: 'They've simply had enough'. And the straw which broke the back of the two Brigadiers— Andre and Ihab? A stunt Ihab Shoukri had tried to pull some three-and-a-half months earlier and which really gave McDonald and his fellow mainstream Brigadiers the hump.

In early March of 2006, Ihab planned to hold a 'show of strength' to show that he was still in charge, even as a surrogate 'brigadier' for his brother. But that attempted bid at bravado backfired: badly and spectacularly.

The plot was to stage the show of strength in The Alexandra Bar, which had been the hub of the Shoukri mob's 'business' operations on Friday nights. But on the Thursday night of 2 March 2006, the PSNI's Serious Crimes Squad decided to 'do the business' on The Alexandra Bar on Belfast's York Road. And, as Chief Constable Sir Hugh Orde would later comment, they were to find that what was going on in the bar that night was 'no teddy bears' picnic'.

———

'Complete mayhem,' was how one startled eyewitness described it. 'It was like something from a *Die Hard* movie.'

Forget Bruce Willis and *Die Hard*. The storming of The Alexandra Bar by the cops was the real thing. It was like something out of a Hollywood blockbuster movie all right. But it was fact—hard fact—not fiction.

Veteran UDA men had long suspected that, because of the mantle of 'The Untouchables', that seemed to place the Shoukris outside the long arm of the law, the brothers themselves were touts.

Now, someone within their own ranks had touted on them, and informed the police about the planned show of strength in The Alexandra pub.

The Shoukris had already been kicked out of the UDA. But the rump of the gang still loyal to the Shoukris, even with Andre behind bars, and who were willing to defy the mainstream UDA, were to be 'honoured' at the show of strength. Ihab had even penned a short script—it didn't amount to a 'speech'—and a 'roll of honour' was to be read out. (Based on this script, he was later to face charges that he wrote it in his own hand, and was a member of both the Ulster Freedom Fighters and the UDA.)

Ihab decided to have a 'rehearsal' for his show of strength on Thursday 2 March. A mini-army of heavily tooled-up cops stormed the Alexandra Bar, the elite of the PSNI's anti-terrorist Mobile Support Units, dressed Ninja-style in black boiler suits, their faces covered in black woollen balaclavas and kitted out in body armour.

It came as no surprise that when the cops went in this time, they went in hard. In the past, well-publicised UDA shows of strength hadn't only involved black berets, black balaclavas and boiler suits. They'd involved guns.

So when the heavily armed peelers stormed The Alexander, they were in no mood for pussyfooting. They went in like the SAS, using CS gas, up to seventy canisters of it. The first of those were fired through smashed windows. The rest followed in a fusillade as police used steel battering rams to hammer in doors.

But, thankfully in terms of police safety, there were no guns inside. And, typically, the seventeen stunned men lifted by police put up no resistance. Indeed, one of the cops later revealed in court documents that Ihab Shoukri himself was found 'huddled against the back fire door'. In other words, well out of the way of any firing line... And we were later told by our sources that one of the so-called 'hard men' had not only lost control of his emotions: he lost control of his bowels!

Significantly, though, another of the special snatch squad of cops said he'd seen a number of men wearing combat trousers and boots—items of illegal paramilitary clothing. And crucially, signed notes were found in the bar, which both the police and prosecutors would later claim were to be used as a speech at the real show of strength on the Friday night.

Ihab Shoukri was among the seventeen men arrested in the police storming of the pub. But there was a gasp of disbelief on the streets when only eleven of those arrested were charged and remanded in custody—and Ihab Shoukri wasn't one of them!

A public outcry followed, clarioned most loudly by nationalist politicians. They, and a host of others—not least within mainstream UDA ranks—believed that the failure to charge Shoukri underpinned their claims that Ihab had for long been a Special Branch tout, and that this was now 'payback' time.

Both the Public Prosecution Service (PPS) and the PSNI came under fierce verbal fire, not least within certain sections of the Press, and certainly by us in *Sunday World*.

Ihab Shoukri was still walking the streets. He was to do so for almost four months. But behind the scenes, police detectives had been squirreling away. They still had the original notes of the handwritten 'speech' which, as it turned out, had been found in the possession of Alan McClean during the riot-squad raid on the bar. And they'd called in a handwriting expert to determine whether the writing matched up to samples previously held of Ihab Shoukri's handwriting. Said a police source at the time: 'It (the speech) was found in somebody else's pocket, but the police have been checking to see who actually wrote it.'

On 28 June 2006, Ihab Shoukri was again arrested. The next day, he was back in court, charged with terrorist offences arising from the raid on the Alexander. By that time, we had already got a fair briefing from our sources of what was in the note allegedly penned by Shoukri.

Our information told us that the statement even tried to turn on its head the infamous quote from Gerry Adams at a republican rally outside Belfast City Hall: 'the IRA haven't gone away, you know'. That was almost exactly the last line in the statement now being attributed to Ihab Shoukri.

As it turned out, the full statement, due to be read at the show of strength on the Friday night of 2 March gave a brief, if slanted, history of the UDA. According to Shoukri's speech, the UDA had evolved into: '... a well-oiled, ruthless killing machine which was name (sic) the Ulster Freedom Fighters. They matched and indeed surpassed the IRA in political assassinations. Some of these volunteers gave many years of their lives in jail, whilst others paid the supreme price with their lives.'

The speech continued: '...Thank you for showing your support tonight. You know now the PIRA has surrendered. This in itself was a victory for the Loyalist community although, our own Unionist politicians and the Secretary of State don't want to seem to give us an consessions (sic).

'So we must now take the fight into the political arena. However, this does not spend (sic) the end for the UDA. We want to reassure you all that the Ulster Defence Association is here to stay.

'I would also like to take this opportunity to let our prisoners and their families know that we will continue to fight for them. And while Hugh Orde calls us criminals and puts only North Belfast Brigade staff in jail on trumped up charges we remain as strong as ever.'

And then came the mimicry of Gerry Adams, with a one-liner in the statement reading: 'We'll never go away you know!!'

The statement concluded, on the 'roll of honour' theme: 'So tonite (sic) we would like to show our appreciation to some of them who have made it here tonite (sic) (get Willie to hand out plaques). Tonite (sic) we would also make a presentation to the North Belfast Brigade on behalf of the volunteers who lost their lives. These men shall never be forgotten.'

A couple of references here are worth noting, in the context of what has since happened. The first is the mention of continuing support for 'our prisoners and their families'. Andre Shoukri was behind bars on remand at the time. The second mentions PSNI Chief Constable Sir Hugh Orde, derogatorily, and accuses him of putting 'only North Belfast Brigade staff in jail on trumped-up charges'.

As it turned out, Andre was not in on 'trumped up' charges and was to cop a guilty plea which earned him a nine-year sentence in pokey, as we have seen. And as for slagging off Hugh Orde, Ihab Shoukri's defence team had been claiming in court that those gathered in The Alexandra bar on the night of the raid were not preparing for a show of strength. Instead, they argued that they had been preparing to announce an end to all UDA crime.

At one stage, a defence lawyer for Ihab Shoukri claimed in court: 'The Chief Constable has sought some sort of gladiatorial contest to pitch himself against the defendant.' He continued that what was happening to his client was 'scandalous', claiming that Shoukri was simply in the bar having a pint when the raid occurred.

The top cop wasn't wearing that one. A marathon runner, he'd put in the hard miles in his quest to put gangsters like Shoukri behind bars. He had put it on the record many times that he did not regard them or the rest of Ulster's paraMafia as anything other than criminal pariahs, preying on their own communities and on society in general.

And the Chief Constable certainly bared his teeth in defence of the raid on The Alexandra Bar, when asked about it at a Press conference staged at a Policing Board meeting in Belfast. Then, he went on the record again with a pointed, if typical, understatement. In one short sentence, he described what was happening in the York Road pub when Shoukri and the other sixteen were scooped there as 'no teddy bears' picnic'.

However, the Judge hearing the case turned out to be no grizzly bear, either. Mr Justice Coghlin didn't exactly savage Shoukri and his sidekick, Alan McClean Jnr, for their part in the illegal show of strength.

Just like his brother Andre had in the extortion case for which he got nine years, Ihab Shoukri let the case drift on and on, repeatedly pleading not guilty to the charge of membership of an illegal organisation, the UDA. Eventually, in May 2008, over two years after the police storming of the Alexandra Bar and just like Andre, Ihab, along with his cohorts, eventually copped a plea of guilty.

Most people expected him to be put away for a long time: membership of an illegal organisation in Northern Ireland carries a maximum sentence of ten years. Shoukri, who took over from his brother as brigadier of the North Belfast Brigade, got just *fifteen months.* When the time already spent on remand on the membership charge was taken into account, he spent just *two months* in jail, following his sentencing in Belfast Crown Court. In fact, he was released in August 2008.

And that, even after the Judge had said in court that the Alexandra Bar escapade was aimed at 'commemorating and glorifying the UDA'.

Mind you, his Honour also couched the lightness of the sentence in the context of what is now happening with the UDA and other paramilitary organisations. Handing down the sentence to both Shoukri and McClean Jnr, the Judge said: 'In my view, it would be unrealistic for the court to close its eyes to the significant changes that have taken place in this society since these offences were committed. It is indisputable that the restoration of local political institutions upon an agreed basis has coincided with the fundamental decline, if not virtual disappearance, of overt terrorist activity carried on by republican and loyalist paramilitaries.'

Well, that observation may be accurate when applied to the mainstream UDA. But Ihab Shoukri had been kicked out of that organisation. The sentence, which would see Shoukri walk in just two months, provoked both public and political outrage. Sinn Féin Stormont Assemblyman and former Mayor of Belfast, Alex Maskey, blasted: 'This case raises serious questions about how loyalists are dealt with by the courts. Lenient sentences send out entirely the wrong message. This type of sentence does nothing to help build the confidence needed in the judicial system.'

And SDLP Assemblyman Alban Maginness, an ex-Lord Mayor of Belfast and a barrister, said he was, 'disappointed at the length' of the Shoukri sentence. He called on the Public Prosecution Service (PPS) to ask the Attorney General in London to 'review the sentence in the light of all the circumstances and to send this case back to the Court of Appeal'.

At the time of writing, the PPS were understood to be considering doing just that.[1]

1. Four weeks before Ihab Shoukri got just fifteen months, he and his brother had reported the PSNI Chief Constable Sir Hugh Orde to the Police Ombudsman. They claimed he had prejudiced their right to a fair trial by publicly claiming in the past that they were leading figures in the UDA. Sir Hugh reacted by bluntly stating: 'I think it's interesting these so-called big men go running to the Ombudsman when we arrest them for very serious offences. I think that's an almost laughable tactic.'

Four weeks later, when he had the handcuffs slapped on him in the dock to be taken down to the cells after being sentenced to that 15-month jail term, Ihab Shoukri smiled over at the knot of his supporters in the Crown Court's public gallery. Little wonder. Undoubtedly, he had the last laugh...

11 | 'NO TEDDY BEARS' PICNIC'

I raised a pint to the storming of The Alexandra when I heard about it. Little wonder. Because in the summer of 2005, Andre Shoukri, aided and abetted by his brother Ihab, had again tried to put the *Sunday World* under the cosh.

He had pushed through a motion at a meeting of the Loyalist Commission sanctioning another, 2003-style 'boycott' (aka campaign of intimidation and terror) against the paper.

Again, I went to the powers-that-be. I contacted the then Secretary of State, Peter Hain, at his Hillsborough-Castle base in County Down. He issued a statement condemning the fresh 'boycott'. Political leaders across the main parties in Northern Ireland did likewise when contacted, just like in 2003.

But in the back channels, I was being told that not all of the UDA leadership—and certainly not the Ulster Volunteer Force bloc on the Loyalist Commission—were behind the Shoukri move this time. Indeed, my sources revealed that the UDA boss, Jackie McDonald, wasn't even at the meeting when the Shoukri motion was 'railroaded' through.

And while Andre Shoukri toured shops on his turf in his BMW the following Sunday, personally warning newsagents not to sell our paper, not one newsagent was approached in McDonald's main base of South Belfast.

So, we were facing down this overt and in-your-face threat again.

And then one appalling incident occurred, the horrendous death of a wee girl, Denise Larkin.

We had been hammering away at the new UDA regime which had taken over from Johnny Adair's notorious C Company on the Shankill Road in Belfast

'Mad Dog', at that stage still languishing in Maghaberry jail while his wife Gina, son Jonathan and the rest of his former 'team' were exiled in Scotland or England, had been replaced by a power-crazy criminal called Charlie Calderwood.

The decent people of the Shankill had hoped that with Adair and his mob out of the way, UDA bosses would impose a new leadership on 'The Road' which would mop up the drug-dealing and criminal legacy of Adair's gangsters. And then, possibly, disband, and give everybody real peace.

Not a bit of it.

Instead, the new Commander on the lower Shankill was Calderwood. And, believe it or not, he was a convicted rapist! So much for 'out with the old, in with the new…'

But worse was to follow. Adair had run his drugs empire from a shebeen in a flute band hall at the back of an old bank off Malvern Street almost opposite the Shankill Leisure Centre. That shebeen was the focus of many complaints that came into our office from the good people of the Shankill—social and community workers and the disgusted parents of kids being subjected to the drugs culture being exploited by C Company.

The community workers told us how young kids of fourteen, fifteen and sixteen years of age could be found lying in doorways the morning after drugs-rich 'raves'—all-night parties where loud dance music blared out—at the shebeen.

The PSNI Chief Constable Sir Hugh Orde had promised a crackdown on paramilitaries, so he ordered crack anti-riot cops to raid the shebeen. I know, because I was there. I got a tip-off that the raid was to take place. We reported the raid—again on the front page—the next day. The shebeen was closed down.

But now, ex-rapist Charlie Calderwood had taken over from Adair on the Lower Shankill. He went one better than a shebeen. He and his C Company hijacked a former ex-Servicemen's club on the Shankill Road. This club was called The Rifles, named after an army regiment. But when Calderwood's mob hijacked it, the voluntary committee running it were powerless to protest when faced with the paramilitaries and it became a drinks and drugs den.

And it cost, directly, the life of Denise Larkin. She was just sweet sixteen. And she died a horrible death—suffering heart attacks and strokes on a life-support machine in hospital after being plied with drugs at a rave in The Rifles. She was reportedly having a relationship with a paramilitary drugs baron in his thirties. He was married and was a top honcho in the Loyalist Volunteer Force in North Belfast. And he had supplied Denise with a deadly cocktail of drugs on that fateful night she died. His name is Laurence 'Duffer' Kincaid. But I'll come back to him later in this book.

As for Denise's premature and prolonged death (she clung on for almost two weeks before the life support machine was switched off) we reported that tragedy, extensively and in grim detail.

Calderwood and his mob 'had it in for us', to put it mildly, not least because we were exposing, week in, week out, fatal incidents like the death of Denise Larkin, which had its roots in

The Rifles club, and every other evil emanating from there, like when we discovered Calderwood's mob's 'Deals on Wheels' service. Fearful for the future of their kids, the decent people on the Shankill again tipped us off—anonymously, of course, for fear of reprisals—that two motorbikes were being used to deliver drugs to 'customers', who simply phoned the club and ordered them.

We confirmed the story from other UDA sources on the Shankill who opposed what Calderwood and his gang were at. And we ran the 'Drug Deals on Wheels' story, harking back to the American movie *Easy Riders*. We dubbed the motorcycle drugs couriers the 'E'-asy Riders: the 'E', of course, representing Ecstasy tablets.

It was stories like that which enraged Calderwood and his sidekick Ebby Irvine, later to take over from Calderwood when, like the 'Bacardi' Brigadier of North Belfast, Charlie's boozing got the better of him. So it came as no surprise when their lower Shankill 'team' backed the Shoukri-sparked 'boycott' of 2005. But this boycott was to endanger the lives of totally innocent people, just because the shop they were working in sold the People's Paper, the *Sunday World*. The newsagents they worked in was located close to the lower Shankill, at Carlisle Circus, situated just at the back of the housing estate which is the base for C Company.

Newsagents on the Shankill had already been visited by 'the boys' and ordered not to sell the paper. But the shop at Carlisle Circus, which also sold groceries, was operating as usual. Until two firebombers stole on to the premises.

The assistants were working at the front of the shop, at the check-outs. All of the Sunday papers were on the racks at the back of the shop, the *Sunday World* as usual, among them. This was an area, fringeing both the Crumlin and Antrim Roads, where our paper sold well. Two hoods from Calderwood's mob on the lower Shankill casually walked into the shop and sprayed petrol over the stacked copies of the *Sunday World*. They then threw matches onto what would become an instant inferno and fled.

The shop assistants working at the front were completely unaware of what had happened, until the smoke from what had become a blaze at the back almost smothered them. They suffered from smoke inhalation. But they were lucky to escape with their lives.

I was in America on a trip organised months before when this happened. The next morning, radio stations back home were clamouring for a reaction. I obliged, and I didn't miss and hit the firewall. I, of course, expressed my sympathy for the staff who had experienced this brush with death, and passed on the wishes of all my staff for their recovery. I also publicly thanked them and the owner of the shop, for continuing to support us through another evil 'boycott'.

But I pointed out, forcefully, that should the perpetrators of this particular crime ever be caught, they should not be charged with arson, a serious crime though that is. I stated emphatically that they should be charged with attempted murder. For if the staff in that shop had not got out in time, it would certainly have been murder.

As it is, no one has ever been arrested or convicted of that crime. But this torching attack was eerily similar to that on the *Sunday World* offices in January 1999, a terrorist incident recorded in my previous book, *Godfathers*. That was carried out by loyalist paramilitary drug-dealers. Petrol was again sprayed around the lobby of our premises and set alight. Fortunately, it was in the dead of night. None of us were in work at the time, but again, the drug Godfathers were trying to exert their own form of censorship: trying to stop the *Sunday World* exposing them and the gangs, and trying but failing to gag the freedom of the press, freedom of expression, and freedom of speech.

However, the ordinary decent people whose letters piled up on my desk week in, week out, wouldn't let the bully boys win. These letters, from both Protestant and Catholic areas, sent a united message. Sub-edited and summed up, it read: 'Please continue the good work in trying to get the jackboot of these fascist paramilitaries off all our backs.'

The spirit of the people and the support they had for us, was summed up in one humorous incident during that Shoukri-led 'boycott' of 2005.

I had gone down to the Cenotaph at Belfast City Hall on Remembrance Sunday, as usual, to watch the wreath-laying ceremony in memory of the dead of the two World Wars and to pay my respects to those brave men and women who had given their lives for their country. I was walking across the City Hall grounds afterwards when I was stopped by a wee woman from the 'Heel 'n'Ankle', the Shankill.

'Jim McDowell, Jim McDowell,' says she as she grabs me by the arm, 'youse all keep up the good work on that paper of yours. Youse are the only ones speaking the truth and exposing these boys for what they really are: drug-dealing scumbags.'

I thanked her for that, and asked where she came from. She said the lower Shankill, right in the heart of C Company's turf.

Now, normally after those Poppy Day ceremonies, I'd go into City Hall and up into the Lord Mayor's parlour for a cup of tea—or something a wee bit stronger—with the Councillors and invited ex-servicemen and women. But as I started walking towards the main gates with this woman, I noticed she walked with a limp. So, I says to this wee woman: 'Missus, you've been very kind to us. I see you're not walking too well. I've got my car parked round the back of the City Hall. Stand here at the front gate; I'll come round and collect you and give you a run up to the bottom of the Shankill.'

Both she and I knew I couldn't give her a lift to her front door. If she was spotted with me—even if any of those dopeheads where out of their beds by that time (around noon) on a Sunday, which was very unlikely—she'd be burned out of her home, despite the fact that she was a pensioner.

However, she spurned the lift. She said she wanted to get a bus. But not up the Shankill—up the Crumlin Road. I asked her why she was going up the Crumlin, and not the Shankill, thinking she was going to a relative for Sunday lunch or something like that.

And it was then the punchline came, which put a smile on my ugly mug for the rest of the Sabbath day and really rammed home the fact that The People's Paper would never lie down under, or be beaten by, these so-called 'boycotts'. Says yer wee wumman: 'Jim, I'm getting the bus up to the Mater Hospital.' Now, the Mater Hospital was originally staffed by Sisters of Mercy and is still recognised as the main 'Catholic' (in quotes) hospital in Belfast.

So I asked this Protestant woman from the Shankill if she was ill, or if she was going to visit someone in the Mater.

Her reply? 'No, not at all. I'm going to the wee shop in the Mater to buy a dozen of your newspapers to put in my handbag and take them round to all the neighbours who have ordered them from me in street where I live.' Here was this brave wee woman, living right in the heart of C Company's territory, where our paper had been banished going to buy it for Protestant people… from a newsagent's stall in a 'Catholic' hospital!

It could only happen in dear oul' Ulster… That wee woman was indeed carrying a big, fit-for-purpose handbag, capable of smuggling in a dozen folded-up *Sunday Worlds*.

But while she had a big handbag, she had also had a big heart.

I thanked her. Hugged her. And had the kind of outsize spring in my step going up the marble steps of the City Hall into the Lord Mayor's parlour for a jar that would have won me an Olympic Gold medal in the high jump...

12 | THE BIG BUST-UP

With Andre Shoukri in jail, and Ihab compromised by his botched show of strength at The Alexandra Bar, Jackie McDonald worked through his 'hoovering' process, 'cleaning up' the ranks, changing the image of the UDA from that of a paramilitary terror gang which preyed on its own communities, to a community-based organisation trying to prise money out of the public purse to aid rundown loyalist areas. Never mind that the UDA had been a major contributory factor, if not *the* major contributory factor, to those areas slipping into deprivation in the first place.

However, McDonald had started building bridges across the Border. His pseudo political wing, the Ulster Political Research Unit (UPRG), was making inroads with both the British and Irish governments, creating dialogue and getting cash to start to set up community structures.

The UDA had tried to engage in real politics at one stage before, setting up the so-called Ulster Democratic Party (UDP), but that had very limited success at the polls, and lasted a very short time before internal schisms torpedoed it. I once asked the veteran socialist, nationalist and avuncular politician Paddy Devlin, a founder member of the Social and Democratic Labour Party (SDLP) with the likes of John Hume and Gerry Fitt, why the UDA's flirtation with politics failed.

Without even blinking, he said to me: 'McDowell, you should know better than anyone. You're a Protestant. And Protestants don't, and won't, vote for gangsters.'

Still, stoking a public and political outcry, the first tranche of the finance promised from public coffers to the UDA was to be £1.2 million, in mid-2006. But that was quickly compromised because of the big internal bust-up within the UDA. Eventually, Stormont Minister Margaret Ritchie was to put the money 'on hold' for a quarantine period of sixty days, during which the UDA had to 'behave itself', or the handout would be cut off. (This was later to become a matter of judicial review in the Ulster High Court and, at the time of writing, has not been resolved.)

McDonald had to act fast. He had got rid of the first two 'Brigadiers of Bling', Adair and Gray, and their terrorist and paraMafia entourages. Now he was moving on the Shoukris. What he was looking for was another internal bloodless coup, just like the sacking of Adair and Gray, but neither Andre Shoukri, in jail, or Ihab, then on the outside, were swallowing this.

The Inner Council decided to act. They ordered a huge rally of their other Belfast Brigades to meet at their Heather Street club base at the top end of the city's Shankill. A massive show of strength ensued.

Ihab Shoukri and his mob were still holed up in the Westland estate, only a mile away across the north of the city. The estate was already hemmed in by tooled-up riot police, the streets blocked off by PSNI armour-plated Land Rovers to prevent any invasion by the mainstream UDA faction and the bloodbath which would surely follow.

Shoukri also had 'scouts' at the top of streets into the estate using walkie-talkie radios to warn of any attacks.

You could have bitten the tension. I know. Myself and our photographer slipped into both areas—unnoticed, it must be said, otherwise we'd have been in big trouble—to take pictures and note what was going on. A friendly cop on duty at the cordon at the Crumlin Road end of the Shankill allowed us to drive through, even though most other cars—other than local residents—were being diverted away from the scene.

The police were also alerted to the mustering of the UDA mainstream, with Jackie McDonald himself present, at Heather Street on the Shankill. They moved quickly to cordon off the area. If a snaking convoy of cars started moving out towards the Westland estate, their orders were to stop it: 'to prevent a breakdown in public order' as the official PSNI jargon had it.

Word filtered through to the Westland estate about what was happening.

We watched from a distance there as the Shoukri mob's top men scurried between houses, while our photographer banged away with a long lens, recording what was happening.

It was now that the third Shoukri brother, Yehia, or Yuk, entered the fray. He has always maintained that he was never a member of the UDA or its killer front, the Ulster Freedom Fighters. But now, as the rump of the Shoukri gang decided to break out of the Westland estate, Yuk made an appearance.

A team of Shoukri heavies slipped through the police cordon. They ghosted out in ones and twos, then they rendezvoused as a mob at the entrance to the nearby Ballysillan housing estate.

A top UDA man, still loyal to the mainstream UDA, lived there. The mob charged up the street where he lived.

Now, this was no mug, no patsy, no easy touch for them. This guy can't be named here for legal reasons, but he was a top UDA hitman. He had a fearsome record inside the organisation. And it was his house the Shoukri rebels targetted.

They had a gun with them, too. Shots were fired. Bullets slammed into his house, but the UDA hitman escaped injury. Yuk Shoukri, who has always insisted he was never in the UDA like his two elder brothers, was one of the leaders of that mob.

Then came the word that the UDA leadership had peremptorily appointed a new Brigadier for North Belfast: right over the Shoukri brothers' heads. His name was John Bunting. And he came from, and lived right in the heart of—the Westland estate!

Ihab and Yuk Shoukri and the 'team', which included other 'heavies' like Tommy 'The Tout' Cousins and Alan McClean disappeared out of the estate, to live under the 'protection' of another UDA breakaway faction, the South-East Antrim Brigade of the UDA.

The huge mob that had mustered at Heather Street on the Shankill had not had to move an inch. The threat of them being there, and the sheer scale of the numbers who had been mobilised against the rump of the Shoukri supporters, was enough. The Heather Street rally, so heavily scrutinised by armed police, broke up peacefully, with many going back to their pints in their nearby clubs without incident.

McDonald had executed another bloodless coup within UDA ranks, just as he had with Jim Gray and Johnny Adair, but booting Ihab Shoukri and those who remained loyal to him and his brother Andre out of North Belfast may have salved one split in the ranks. It also created a much bigger and much deeper chasm.

When McDonald had made his move against Jim Gray in East Belfast, Andre Shoukri had abstained when it came to the crunch vote at the Inner-Council meeting to stand down and court-martial 'Doris Day'. Throughout the weeks-long tussle to topple the Shoukris, there was a re-run of that abstention. And it involved one of the largest blocs of the whole UDA organisation, the South-East Antrim Brigade.

Its fiefdom stretched from the sprawling Rathcoole housing estate—at one time the biggest of its kind in Western Europe—on the northern boundaries of Belfast, up the coast to Carrick-fergus, where the Protestant hero King Billy landed by boat in 1690, on up to the ferry port of Larne, across to the mid-Antrim town of Ballyclare (where Andre Shoukri had bought a luxury house with money that hadn't gone over the bookies' counter) and up to Ian Paisley's 'Bible Belt' capital of Ballymena.

It corralled thousands of men in its ranks and its former Brigadier had been an extremely high-profile 'hard man', John 'Grug' Gregg. A shaven-headed base drummer in a loyalist flute band, he had presided over a brigade which had been responsible for a brutal catalogue of sectarian murders, not the least of which was the dawn gunning-down of innocent Catholic twenty-year-old Danny McColgan as he reported for work as a postman at a Royal Mail depot near Gregg's Rathcoole lair.

But Gregg himself was to be gunned down during the internal UDA feud which saw Johnny Adair being deposed. It was Gregg who had sent Andre Shoukri out of the Rathcoole estate in 2002 to shoot 'Mad Dog' Adair. But in 2003, Adair's supporters got their own back.

Shoukri, as reported earlier, had been caught by cops with a gun on the fringes of the estate, but later, strangely, had his first, heavy jail sentence reduced when his lawyers appealed, claiming Shoukri himself was under a death threat from Adair's C Company, and was carrying the weapon for his own protection. It was that incident which sparked the assassination of John 'Grug' Gregg, once jailed himself for a botched assassination bid on Gerry Adams.

Andre Shoukri as a 14-year-old wannabe soccer star at the Boys' Model School in Belfast. He wanted to play for Arsenal—the Gunners. The closest he got to that was carrying a gun—and getting caught!

Andre, again. This time, decked out in tuxedo and bow-tie—before the gangly youth became the gangster dubbed 'The Bookies' Brigadier'.

The Shoukri smirk has gone in this picture, smuggled out of HM Prison Maghaberry. Instead, it's a sultry and sullen Andre… bulked up from bodybuilding, but behind bars: where he belongs.

The other 'main man' in *The Mummy's Boys*—Ihab Shoukri. He's seen here (centre, in Red Bull motorbike racing jacket) leaving court with his cronies. But, just like his brother, he eventually copped a plea… and ended up behind bars, too.

Some threats officially notified to me by the police: from both sides, and directed at me, my family, and the *Sunday World* staff.

CMC Ref No. ....

POLICE MESSAGE – CASTLEREAGH DCU

Name:	SON OF JIM MCDOWELL
Address:	....
Message:	POLICE HAVE RECEIVED INFORMATION THAT MEMBERS OF LVF INTEND TO CARRY OUT AN ATTACK ON A PERSON BELIEVED TO BE THE SON OF JIM MCDOWELL EDITOR OF THE SUNDAY WORLD. THIS ATTACK MAY BE RELATED TO HIS EMPLOYMENT.

Delivered by:

Name .... Rank: ....

Station: .... Date: .... Time: ....

Location of delivery ....

Received by:

Name: .... Date: ....

Police / Recipient / Cross Copy* Delete Accordingly

The police warning of the evil threat against Jamie, which forced us to get him out of the country. It came from Duffer Kincaid's LVF mob—and, as the front page carried here shows, drugs Godfather Kincaid, pictured on the right of page 1, was no stranger to the *Sunday World*.

The front page which sparked the 2003 loyalist paramilitary 'boycott'—in reality a campaign of terror and intimidation—against the *Sunday World*. UDA drugs Godfather Jim 'Doris Day' Gray was behind it. The headline proved prophetic: he was later shot dead by his former best buddy.

SUNDAY WORLD

■ VOL 31 ■ NO 1 MARCH 23, 2003 £1.00

9 770791 677064

THE PEOPLE'S PAPER

SIEGE OF BAGHDAD

BRITISH and American bombs blitzed Baghdad again last night, as large parts of Iraq fell into Allied control.

Missiles launched from American ships and Royal Navy submarines hit strategic targets in the city.

Four US soldiers were killed after being ambushed by Iraqi troops and six British servicemen were killed in a mid-air collision between two helicopters, pushing the UK death toll to 14.

See Pages 6,7,8,9,10,11&36

BURNING OIL FIELDS: Royal Irish Regiment soldiers in Iraq last night

PUSHING ON: British Army soldiers peer into a trench where two dead Iraqis held a white flag

THE MAN WHO TRIED TO GAG YOUR SUNDAY WORLD

CENSORED: Reverend Mervyn Gibson sanctioned a boycott campaign against the Sunday World

Top loyalist pastor OK's campaign of lies, threats

By JIM McDOWELL, Northern Editor

THE Sunday World has been the target of a vicious campaign of lies and threats this week. And this is the man who rubberstamped it. He's the Rev. Mervyn Gibson, who calls himself a Christian clergyman. But he is the head of the so-called Loyalist Commission, which includes terrorist bosses.

FULL REPORTS and COMMENT: Pages 2&3

The ex-RUC Special Branch cop-turned-clergyman, the Reverend Mervyn Gibson. He was head of the Loyalist Commission which sanctioned the 'boycott': so we put him on the front page, too. He didn't like it…

Drug-dealers and gangsters had targeted the *Sunday World* before. They torched our office in 1999. Then Secretary of State Mo Mowlam visited to show solidarity. Martin O'Hagan, our colleague, is pictured on the extreme right. Two years later, he was murdered by the drugs paraMafia mob known as the Loyalist Volunteer Force.

LVF founder and Godfather Billy 'King Rat' Wright, pictured under a makeshift 'Orange' arch inside the old Maze jail. While alive, he ordered that if anything happened to him, Martin O'Hagan was to be shot in revenge. Along with other *Sunday World* journalists, Martin continually exposed Wright and his terror gang's criminal and murderous underworld.

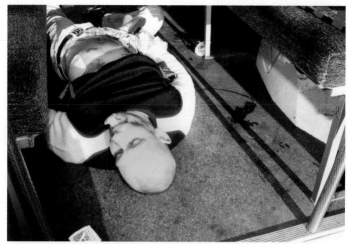

Wright was shot dead behind bars just after Christmas 1997. We ran the picture of Wright lying dead in a prison van on the front page. That got us into more trouble…

INLA murderer Christopher 'Crip' McWilliams, whose gang gunned down 'King Rat' inside the jail. He was later to die of cancer: but we revealed that this hard-hearted, ruthless republican killer had visited Lourdes… in search of a miracle cure to keep him alive.

Self-confessed loyalist killer Michael Stone, pictured here in a flak jacket, never gave the *Sunday World* 'flak'. But he did tell us how he had stalked both Gerry Adams and Martin McGuinness—even before he tried to murder them, first at the funeral of the Gibraltar Three at Milltown cemetery in March 1988; then in his solo storming of the Stormont Assembly nineteen years later.

Working for—and with—the *Sunday World* can be dangerous. This picture proves it. We exposed the two drug-dealers pictured here—Brendan 'Speedy' Fegan (*left*) and Brendan Campbell—living the high life in the back of a hired limousine. Both were later gunned down on the orders of the Provos, by an IRA front gang dubbed Direct Action Against Drugs (DAAD). And the source who supplied us with this picture was later killed in cold blood, too...

The paramilitaries mighn't have liked us, and tried to shut us up—one way or the other. But a lot of people kept talking to the *Sunday World*, as this selection of front pages shows…

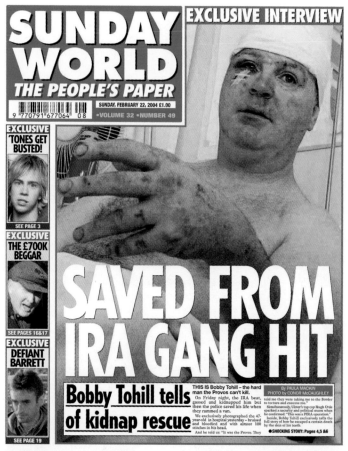

EXCLUSIVE INTERVIEW

SUNDAY WORLD
THE PEOPLE'S PAPER

SUNDAY, FEBRUARY 22, 2004 £1.00
•VOLUME 32 •NUMBER 49

9 770791 677064 08

EXCLUSIVE
'TONES GET BUSTED!
SEE PAGE 3

EXCLUSIVE
THE £700K BEGGAR
SEE PAGES 16&17

EXCLUSIVE
DEFIANT BARRETT
SEE PAGE 19

SAVED FROM IRA GANG HIT

Bobby Tohill tells
of kidnap rescue

THIS IS Bobby Tohill – the hard man the Provos can't kill.
On Friday night, the IRA beat, gassed and kidnapped him but then the police saved his life when they rammed a van.

We exclusively photographed the 47-year-old in hospital yesterday – bruised and bloodied and with almost 100 stitches in his head.

And he told us: "It was the Provos. They

By PAULA MACKIN
PHOTO by CONOR McCAUGHLEY

told me they were taking me to the Border to torture and execute me."

Simultaneously, Ulster's top cop Hugh Orde sparked a security and political storm when he confirmed: "This was a PIRA operation."

Inside, Bobby Tohill exclusively tells the full story of how he escaped a certain death by the skin of his teeth.

●SHOCKING STORY: Pages 4,5 &6

Belfast hardman Bobby Tohill—who once boasted to us that he had been a terrorist since the age of twelve—was left battered and bloodied by a gang who tried to kidnap and kill him. But from his hospital bed the next day, he told us: 'It was the Provos. They told me they were taking me to the Border to torture and execute me.'

The UDA's first 'Brigadier of Bling', Jim 'Doris Day' Gray, didn't only fall out with us. He fell out with his ex-wife, Anne Tedford—and she spilled the beans on how Gray had left the couple's son to die alone in a hotel room in Thailand… surrounded by hookers.

Evil rapist rang girl's mum after sick attack

EXCLUSIVE
by PAULA MACKIN

A TEEN rapist rang his victim's mother to boast about his sickening attack.

A 15-year-old girl from London was the victim of a sickening double rape in Belfast in the early ours of yesterday morning.

The child victim's friends were forced to watch as she was subjected to an horrific attack at the hands of an opportunist attacker believed to be 16-18 years of age.

Gut-wrenching details of the assault in west Belfast emerged yesterday.

Ordeal

The girl was raped in the forecourt of a garage on Blacks Road - the rapist's accomplice threatened the victim's three friends and forced them to watch.

The attackers were armed with a metal bar and a screwdriver.

The girl and her friends were robbed of money and their mobile phones before being dragged into the garage forecourt.

Her ordeal was only starting.

Despite her screams for help she was dragged to the nearby Colin Valley Golf Centre where the terrified schoolgirl was raped for the second time – again her friends were forced to watch.

When he had finished the sick rapist used his victim's phone to ring her mother and boast of his perverted deeds.

FULL STORY: Page 14

EXCLUSIVE INTERVIEW

SHOUKRI SPEAKS ONLY TO THE SUNDAY WORLD

By JIM McDOWELL

THE UFF boss blamed for trying to ban the *Sunday World* from loyalist areas has given an exclusive interview – to this newspaper!

In a bizarre twist, north Belfast UFF 'Brigadier' Andre Shoukri (above) contacted us this week.

He DENIED he was behind a terror campaign of threat and intimidation to stop ordinary people in loyalist areas reading this paper.

He said he had phoned to REBUT what was written about him in last week's paper – even though it is supposed to be banned on his own 'turf'.

But he point-blank REFUSED to discuss any details of any meetings he was at with either the UFF or the UVF.

And in another bolt out of the blue, Shoukri echoed the recent statement from the IRA when he said of the UDA/UFF: "We want peace!"

FULL BIZARRE INTERVIEW: Pages 4&5

COLOMBIAN THREE USED FAKE PASSPORTS TO GET BACK HOME! Turn to Pages 8&9

The one-time wannabe soccer star Andre Shoukri scored a spectacular own goal—when he broke his own boycott of the *Sunday World* and phoned me to complain about what we were writing about him! You can see the treatment we gave it, on the front page. Again, he wasn't amused…

Top Provo and Sinn Féin frontman Denis Donaldson did a runner to
Donegal after confessing to having been a British superspy for over twenty
years. But when the *Sunday World* tracked him down to his hovel hideaway,
he talked to us… before being shot dead at his own door days later.

The UDA, and the Shoukris in particular, had tried to put us off the streets. But then, the UDA kicked the Shoukris out and decided to put themselves off the streets… and we ran the exclusive front page of their plans—THREE WEEKS before it was officially announced, on Remembrance Sunday, 11 November 2007. There were still those within their ranks leaking stories to us…

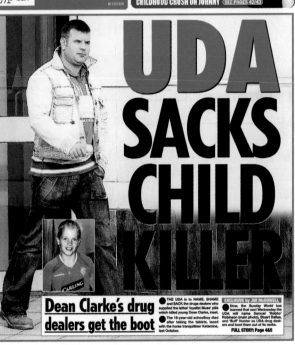

Time and time again, often under threat, we'd exposed drug-dealers in the UDA and in the ranks of other paraMafia mobs. But it took the death of a 16-year-old schoolboy, Dean Clarke, to kick-start UDA bosses into action—and to kick out a whole drug-dealing gang, as this front page shows.

The UDA subscribed to the maxim: 'Proud to be a Prod'. But they, too, could take the mickey—as was proved by this graffiti about me on shutters in the loyalist heartland of Sandy Row. The *Sunday Life* is, of course, our main newspaper rival in Belfast. I must admit, I had a chuckle or two when I saw it... (*Alan Lewis*)

On the night of Saturday 1 February 2003, when he had just got off a boat back from Scotland after watching his beloved Glasgow Rangers football team, Gregg sat in a taxi on his way home to Rathcoole with one of his main lieutenants, Rab Carson. He was ambushed by assassins ordered by Adair: even 'though 'Mad Dog' was still behind bars at the time and has since denied to me in interviews that he had anything to do with the murder.

Even by Ulster standards, it was an audacious murder mission, smacking of that old cliché, an Al-Capone-style Chicago killing. A car rammed the taxi carrying Gregg and Carson through the dimly lit docks area of Belfast. Two gunmen jumped out. They riddled Gregg and Carson with bullets. Both died instantly. Pictures of them lying bloodied and lifeless in the back seat of the taxi were to appear in Monday morning's papers, as the killing happened too late on the Saturday night for most of the Sundays.

That double murder sealed the fate of Adair and his mob. It led directly to the forcing out of his family and the rump of his supporters still left in the lower Shankill, and their flight to the boat to Scotland under heavily armed police escort.

However, 'Grug' Gregg's South-East Antrim (SEA) Brigade had been heavily steeped in drugs, protection rackets, armed robberies, and, of course, killing, mainly of innocent Catholics like young Danny McColgan. We reported those criminal activities frequently. So Gregg wasn't a fan of mine, or of anybody else in the *Sunday World*. And he made that clear at the funeral of one loyalist paramilitary feud victim in North Belfast.

I was there reporting on the funeral. As he passed by in the cortege, what Gregg called me is unprintable here. Let's just say I would never have been asked to join him for a pint at his local, the Cloughfern Arms pub, later torched during yet another loyalist internecine vendetta.

Still, with 'Grug' Gregg gone, the UDA drafted in a replacement brigadier, Gary Fisher. Unlike the highly physical and highly visible Gregg, Fisher was, and still is, the UDA version of The Invisible Man. Newspaper 'morgues', or libraries, in Belfast have portfolios full of photographs of the main UDA 'players', but Fisher isn't in any of them. Even though during Gregg's time as brigadier in South-East Antrim (SEA) Fisher was the main man in that brigade's lucrative drug-running operation. He even sited the SEA mob's main drugs depot—where truckloads of drugs were brought to be split up and then dispatched—in a warehouse close to the boating marina at Ballyronan, smackdab in the middle of the IRA heartland of South Derry, around the shores of Lough Neagh!

Fisher was also on a nice little earner himself. Never mind him not appearing in any newspaper picture portfolios, we also discovered that he and his sidekick, Tommy 'Millions' Kirkham, who earned his nickname for reasons I'll explain shortly, hold a considerable personal property portfolio between them. Fisher owns at least three houses, and he and Kirkham even have an 'option' on a plot of land immediately adjacent to the UDA's biggest drinking club, the Eastways club in the heart of their Rathcoole base.

Kirkham had always been close to the UDA leadership. He'd been one of the instigators and leading figures in their original political party, the Ulster Democratic Party (UDP). He'd also been key to the founding of the Ulster Political Research Group. He'd been one of their main spokesmen. And, in spite of my late friend Paddy Devlin's acerbic assertion that 'Protestants don't vote for gangsters', Kirkham had run, and been elected in, the local government elections in the borough of Newtownabbey, which covers a large patch of the SEA Brigade's 'turf'.

He's still a councillor there.

But both he and his Brigadier, Fisher, would fall foul of the UDA mainstream during the rift which led to the expulsion and downfall of the Shoukris. Just as when Shoukri abstained in the Jim Gray expulsion vote, Fisher and Kirkham, business partners of the Shoukris in the lucrative drugs racket, opted to abstain—or, as they put it, 'remain neutral'—as the Inner Council dealt with the 'Shoukri problem'. And the rift was to run even deeper when the SEA Brigade gave shelter to Ihab Shoukri and his top henchmen. That in turn would lead eventually to Fisher and Kirkham's expulsion from the UDA—and the whole of the SEA Brigade with them.

And to more threats coming my way.

13 | THE DIRTY DOZEN

Tommy Kirkham was just plain Tommy Kirkham when he was the main mouthpiece for the SEA Brigade run by the now-deceased brigadier John 'Grug' Gregg.

He had been a flag-bearer for the now-defunct political party, the Ulster Democratic Party, set up as the UDA's political wing under the leadership of Gary McMichael, son of another UDA brigadier, John McMichael, himself murdered by the IRA when they planted a 'magnet', or booby-trap bomb, under his car on 22 December 1987.

As it turned out, John McMichael—who, ironically, had co-produced a pamphlet 'Commonsense' while alive which made the first move towards pointing the UDA away from violence—was 'Judassed', set up, by one of his own. The Judas in this case was former UDA bully boy and freeloading, freelancing gangster, Jimmy Craig.

Craig, like the Shoukris, Gray and Adair who came after him, dripped in gold jewellery and lived a flash lifestyle. And just like Andre Shoukri, he was trousering a sizeable whack of the money that was supposed to be going into UDA coffers. John McMichael tasked a special squad to probe Craig's activities.

But Craig had connections in the Provos. He had been oper-ating through a go-between known as 'The Fixer' to split up protection rackets with the IRA on building sites throughout Belfast: agreeing which terror gang should 'put the bee' (the sting) on which building contractors, and where.

A classic case was the construction of the Westlink dual carriageway linking the M2 Motorway from the north of Belfast to the M1 Motorway heading south to Dublin. This motorway passed through both Protestant and Catholic areas. And the entire length of the link road was split up between the respec-tive paramilitaries 'almost inch by inch', according to one senior cop serving in west Belfast at the time.

John McMichael, Jackie McDonald's predecessor as brigadier for South Belfast, had put Craig's mainly self-serving criminal activities under the microscope. And Craig did not take matters like that lightly.

I know. I was reporting on the funeral of one of Belfast's best-known characters, one of the old-timers, 'Silver' McKee, who only fought with his fists in legendary bare-knuckle street battles, when Craig and his sidekick 'Artie' Fee drove past.

The funeral was taking place at one of Belfast's most beauti-ful old Catholic Churches, St Malachy's, at the back of the Market area of Belfast where 'Silver' McKee had lived and worked as a cattle drover in the livestock market.

A huge crowd had gathered, both inside and outside the chapel.

I was covering it for radio, and doing a running commentary for the news bulletins. I was standing talking to a 'wide boy' outside—let's just call him 'Big Seamie'—who was one of the many hundreds who had come to pay their last respects to this street-fighting hard man.

Now I knew 'Big Seamie' had already had a number of run-ins with Jimmy Craig. The former had been one of the first 'entrepreneurs' to start 'massage parlours' in Belfast, a cover name for brothels. They had sprung up in respectable areas in a religion-haunted, Bible-thumping city where in the past brothels had only operated up side alleys, or 'entries' as they are known in Ulster: Pottinger's Entry in downtown Belfast being a prime case in point.

Craig had tried to muscle in on the massage-parlour business. Not just trying to squeeze protection money out of it, but setting up as a pimp. But 'Big Seamie' had a few paramilitary connections himself, on the other side of the fence from Craig. Threats had passed both ways and a few spats. However, no-one had ended up on a pathologist's cold marble slab… yet.

But as I was yarning to 'Big Seamie', he suddenly glanced down the street, hissed out two words, 'F**k me!', and took off like one of the greyhounds he reared.

Looking back now, the sight of his big long, lanky legs flailing like the sails of a windmill as he sprinted down Alfred Street and round the nearest corner seems funny. It wasn't then. For when I looked down the street in the direction 'Big Seamie' had glanced before suddenly taking fright, I saw a Ford Capri car which slowly crawled up Adelaide Street like a crocodile cruising towards a deer drinking at a riverbank.

I recognised that car instantly. A lot of other people at that funeral did so too.

'Silver McKee was never 'connected': to the Provos or any other paramilitaries. His funeral was supposed to be sacrosanct: everyone who attended, even though they may have been 'connected', was to be accorded safe passage for the day.

But here was Jimmy Craig cruising up the street slowly, past the packed ranks of mourners gathered outside the chapel.

'Big Seamie' obviously thought Craig was there for him, and he'd be the next in a coffin. But I didn't think he'd even eyeballed 'Big Seamie' taking to his heels. Craig, with his sidekick Artie Fee 'riding shotgun' as usual in the front passenger seat of the Capri, just drove past, slowly and deliberately, making sure everyone knew he was there.

It was impossible not to. And it seemed to me at the time that Craig was putting his own fingerprint on 'Silver's' funeral. It was as if he was paying a personal, silent, but very high-profile, 'mark of respect'.

I didn't report that on the radio bulletins that day, but I planned to hold that line for Sunday. Before then, however, I made my own inquiries from my UDA contacts, especially on the Shankill Road, where Craig lived and from where he operated.

Inevitably, Craig got to hear of the 'mark-of-respect' line I was thinking of running on his surprise, if prominent, appearance at the McKee funeral. He phoned the office. And he warned me, 'Don't be writing that load of s***e.'

'Why not?' I asked.

'Just don't be writing it, I'm tellin' you,' came the gravelly-voiced grunt.

'But I'm told you were at Silver's funeral to pay your respects, one hard man to another,' I said.

'Why I was there is none of your f*****g business. And I wasn't there to pay any respects. So, as I said, don't be writing any of that s***e, or I'll be down to see you…' And with that thinly veiled threat hanging in the air, he hung up.

As it turned out, I didn't write the story. Because my contacts on the Shankill came back to me. And they confirmed that Craig hadn't been at the McKee funeral to pay his 'last respects' after all. Instead, as he'd correctly guessed, he'd been there to hasten the Last Rites for someone else. Big Seamie.

As it was, just like 'Silver' McKee, Jimmy Craig wasn't to be long for this life either.

For some time he had been suspected, by his own side, of setting up two other loyalist assassination victims for republican connections. One was Lenny Murphy, the leader of the bunch of UVF psychopaths who gained bloody infamy as the Shankill Butchers. Murphy was gunned down by the Provos outside his home at the top of the Shankill in November 1982.

The other was firebrand loyalist politician and Belfast City Councillor George Seawright, gunned down by a veteran Irish National Liberation Army assassin as he sat in a taxi close to the Shankill on 19 November 1987.

Seawright, originally from Glasgow, had been getting close to blowing the gaffe on Craig's self-enriching gangsterism: as had John McMichael and his special internal UDA investigation squad. Both paid with their lives. But it was the killing of McMichael which signed Craig's death warrant.

Craig was summoned to east Belfast for a meeting, ironically in the same bar, the Bunch of Grapes, which Jim 'Doris Day' Gray co-owned and was later to have Geordie Legge butchered in. The UDA's main headquarters were situated in the East of the city, in Gawn Street, not far away from the Bunch of Grapes.

Craig was standing drinking at the bar on a Saturday night, in October 1988, when a gunman walked in and shot him dead. It was a bloodbath. His sidekick Artie Fee, standing right beside Craig, escaped unscathed. Not one bullet even winged him. And today, there is still scepticism in UDA ranks about the cold-blooded killing. Had Jimmy Craig, who had 'Judassed' so many people in the past, been finally 'Judassed' himself?

And what's the 'Judas' connection in relation to Tommy 'Millions' Kirkham? Simply this, when the UDA leadership, under McDonald, moved to remove the Shoukris from north Belfast, they felt that Kirkham and the SEA Brigadier Gary Fisher had 'Judassed' the parent body, the mainstream UDA, by refusing to go along with the sacking of the Shoukris. The UDA hierarchy were well aware of the strong 'business bonds'

between the Shoukri mob and the so-called 'Dirty Dozen'—
including Fisher and Kirkham—who spearheaded the SEA
Brigade and shared the spoils among themselves.

And the Shoukris' business with the 'Dirty Dozen' can be
summed up in one word: drugs.

So when these men adopted a 'neutral stance' over the sacking of the Shoukris, 'The Dirty Dozen'—and Kirkham in
particular—had their cards marked by the rest of the Inner
Council. But Kirkham thought he wielded a lot of power—
albeit within 'the organisation': decent people outside it
despised him and what he espoused—and, as Ulster folk would
say, he was capable of 'running away with himself'. In other
words, he was capable of making big gaffes. Like the time he
was ordered by Gregg to contact TV and radio stations to
correct their news reports that the Red Hand Defenders, yet
another pseudonym used by UDA assassination squads, were
responsible for a particularly grisly sectarian murder. Kirkham
rang up one TV station to say that their report was inaccurate:
it was, in fact, the UDA/UFF who had carried out the killing.
And he did it from a public phone box. Which was traceable.
But, again surprisingly—or maybe not given that so many
paramilitary gangs in Ulster were peppered with touts—
Kirkham didn't end up in jail.

Still, along with other UDA veterans like Sammy Duddy from
Rathcoole and Frankie Gallagher from East Belfast, Kirkham
had been part of UPRG delegations which met and negotiated
with politicians from both sides of the border. He had even met
Ulster Secretaries of State to put the evolving and unfolding
UDA/UPRG 'community-based' strategy and case. He was an
integral part of the paramilitary politburo that was supposed
to be taking the UDA away from violence and crime and down
the road to a community-based organisation, if it was not yet

ready or willing to take to the polls as a full-blown political entity, like Sinn Féin had for the Provos.

All of that was to end when the South-East Antrim Brigade refused to back the Inner Council over the expulsion of the Shoukris. A 'Cold War' broke out between the remaining five UDA brigades and their former SEA allies. And what was, at the outset, a war of words between the McDonald and Kirkham camps quickly heated up. Accusations were flying between the former bedfellow brigades.

I know. I was being constantly briefed by a very senior UPRG member who was right inside the McDonald camp.

Documents detailing the past 'misdemeanours' of the SEA leadership—Fisher's and Kirkham's—were being regularly passed on to me at these 'meets' and it was during these briefings that the concept of the 'Dirty Dozen', who had led—or in the mainstream's parlance 'railroaded'—the whole of the massive SEA Brigade into outright rebellion against the rest of the Inner Council, first surfaced.

The line here was that this 'Dirty Dozen', an inner clique in the SEA Brigade, had all personally benefited from crimes committed in the UDA's name, had close 'business' ties to the Shoukris, and were the main culprits behind the major split. Fisher and Kirkham were ID'd as the top two in the damning dossiers.

We are the newspaper with the biggest sale into the Protestant working-class housing estates where these boys were running their writ, and when we ran these stories, which exposed the internal workings of a brigade in Ulster's biggest paraMafia, Kirkham and Co. didn't like it. We knew this because people calling themselves 'veterans' from the SEA Brigade, who had objected to the split, were contacting us to tell us.

Kirkham himself was publicly irked. He was briefing rival newspapers, giving his side of the story, but again, he 'ran away with himself' and made a huge public-relations gaffe, very much in the public eye, too.

It began when the UDA let it be known that Kirkham and Fisher were now *personae non grata* with the Inner Council: they were sacked. The 'Dirty Dozen' of their cronies were 'stood down' too, but without any big public statement.

One of the main reasons for the sackings by the Inner Council was that the SEA Brigade was sheltering Ihab Shoukri, who had slunk off from his north-Belfast hinterland to live in the SEA Brigade's territory, setting up with some of his cronies in a little hamlet in Islandmagee, near the port of Larne in Co. Antrim.

True to form, they were travelling into and strutting about Larne every day, and visiting one venue in particular for some R&R: not that any of them needed it. None of them had ever done a decent day's work in their lives. But our contacts up in Larne—again, contacts within the ranks of the SEA Brigade—were telling us that the venue they were visiting on a daily basis was—you've guessed it!—the 'cream cookies', the bookies.

And they were still dealing in drugs. In fact, we revealed at one stage that one of Ihab Shoukri's new 'partners' in that sleazy business (now in the heart of Ulster's Bible Belt, at that) was a Catholic and that his family had serious republican connections.

The fact that Shoukri and his exiles from north Belfast were running about so openly on the rebel SEA Brigade's patch and flaunting their presence there seriously pissed off the Inner Council. In yet another briefing document given to us through the back channels they were using, the Council accused Fisher and Kirkham's breakaway Brigade of 'giving shelter and succour' to the rump of the Shoukri mob. They accused the SEA Brigade of taking them 'under their wing'.

But the Inner Council didn't want another guns-blazing, blow-their-balls-off internal feud. For one thing, they couldn't afford it. They were still trying to change the face, or in some people's eyes, the façade, of the UDA, and were punting for public money (that £1.2 million for a start) from the government via the Stormont Assembly. They had got rid of Gray, Adair and the Shoukris in bloodless coups.

They calculated that there would be a grassroots rebellion among SEA Brigade ranks when they expelled, and then exposed, the 'Dirty Dozen'. Within days of Fisher, Kirkham and Co. being booted out, sources within the Inner Council were claiming that a groundswell of opposition to the 'Dirty Dozen' had begun in their own SEA Brigade ranks.

That's when Kirkham made his big PR gaffe. It was a classic case of someone putting his (in this case financial) foot in his mouth. He called a Press conference in a Carrickfergus hotel, timed for a Monday morning: deliberately so, so that we in the *Sunday World* would miss it. Not that we would have expected to be invited, anyway, given the circumstances. And as it happened, we weren't.

At the Press conference, Kirkham unveiled a ramp of new proposals from the SEA Brigade, including poster campaigns, for fighting crime and combating the 'drugs problem' in its area. A 'community-based' ethos was also expounded, at length. And in an attempt to upstage the Inner Council—who were still insisting that, in spite of the cash coming from the Government, decommissioning of UDA weapons was 'not on the horizon'—Kirkham said that the UDA in South-East Antrim could be disbanded within three years.

To this end, Kirkham also launched a new propaganda pamphlet at the Carrick conference, entitled 'Beyond Conflict'. Then he put a price on peace which not only stunned the seasoned hacks gathered at the Press conference, it simply appalled the public, many of whom were already railing and raging at the government plan to backhand that £1.2 million to the mainstream UDA.

With a brass neck the size of ex-World Champ boxer Mike Tyson's, Kirkham blatantly and publicly asked the Government for *eight-and-a-half million pounds*, for the SEA Brigade to go away, in what was clearly an act of blackmail.

That blew up in his face, big time. The following Sunday we suggested another title for the 'Beyond Conflict' pamphlet. It wasn't complimentary; we dubbed it 'Beyond Belief.' That stuck, and again according to our sources inside the SEA Brigade, it stuck right up Tommy Kirkham's nose.

What's more, after he had asked for that incredible eight-and-a-half million quid of taxpayers' money, we also ran a story about Kirkham's and Fisher's personal, and joint, property portfolios worth millions. And we 'christened' Kirkham Tommy 'Millions' Kirkham in print. Said one of our prime contacts within the SEA Brigade: 'He went ballistic at that…'

Both he and Fisher were also going ballistic about growing dissent within SEA ranks over the split with the mainstream UDA. The 'Dirty Dozen' were issuing threats to dissidents within the SEA Brigade who opposed the split. And Ihab Shoukri was stirring the pot—as well as selling it. Sources within the re-vamped North Belfast Brigade let it be known that he was issuing death threats to those who had deposed him and his brother.

Tension peaked on two occasions, boiling over into a white-knuckle stand-off on July 21 2007 that almost saw Jackie McDonald shot as the bullets flew, and which resulted in the shooting of a police officer.

Three months earlier, on April 29, we ran a story that the mainstream UDA had put all its brigades on 'stand-by'. These included all the Belfast brigades, and the 'Londonderry' outfit covering most of Derry run by Billy 'The Mexican' McFarland.

This tip-off, too, had come from our by-now-established senior source within the Inner Council.

The story was that this could be a re-run of the Heather Street rally, when it looked like the UDA were going to invade the Westland-estate stronghold of the Shoukris, physically to oust them. This time, the word was the UDA had put a blueprint in place to invade the massive Rathcoole estate, the heartland of the SEA Brigade.

When they read the story, Kirkham and Fisher panicked. They thought the 'invasion' was going to take place that afternoon, so they ordered all their 'troops' to muster on 'The Green'—a vast, open space in the middle of Rathcoole—that afternoon. And, upping the odds, they invited Ihab Shoukri and his cronies along.

Now, they weren't only 'sheltering' them, as claimed by the Inner Council. They were showboating them. They claimed that a crowd of two thousand turned up. The mainstream UDA claimed it was 'only in the hundreds'.

The showdown with the mainstream Brigades didn't happen. It later transpired it was never scheduled for that Sunday, anyway, and in the paper, we hadn't referred to a date. But it showed that the old barbed-wire-in-the-blood was spikey among Kirkham's mob. As one source said: 'Their oul' Bangor Reserves—their nerves—are certainly on edge.'

So much so, that a second incident occurred, which further exacerbated the tension running between the mainstream and the rebel factions.

Not every member of the SEA Brigade ordered to turn up at the Rathcoole mustering obeyed. There was a growing band of dissidents within the rebel brigade still loyal to McDonald's parent body and who hankered after a reunion.

The 'Dirty Dozen' decided to make an example of one of them. A 'Romper Room' squad reminiscent of the really bad

old days of the UDA burst into the home of one young man—
not a 'veteran', just an objector—and gave him a terrible beating.
He ended up in hospital with horrendous injuries.

We tried to speak to him, but he wouldn't talk to us. He was
frightened for members of his family still living in Rathcoole.

That incident was further to stoke the ire of the Inner
Council. And it was to spark a string of incidents—including
that near-death gun incident involving McDonald—which are
still unfolding at the time of writing.

As for my own take on the whole 'rebel Brigade' and Tommy
'Millions' Kirkham saga. Well, that was a classic case of the shit
hitting 'the ban'. As you've probably detected, I'm no fan of his.
And yes, it's personal, as well as professional. It's a matter of
principle: he made money out of the terrorism which took
people's lives and which I have always, and continue, to abhor.

After the so-called 'boycott' of our newspaper in 2003, sanctioned by the Loyalist Commission, a senior UDA source told
me that Kirkham and another top mouthpiece at the time later
smirked: 'Sure, that was only to scare the shite out of big
McDowell…'

It didn't. But consider, this remark came after a senior police
officer had visited my home and advised me strongly to get
myself and my family out of the country because Jim 'Doris
Day' Gray was sending gunmen to shoot me. And Kirkham was
later to smirk about all of this? Aye, long runs the fox.

14 | THE SECRET FILES THAT SANK THE SHOUKRIS

In the past, the UDA has done neither me, nor the *Sunday World* staff, any favours. But what a difference a 'Doris Day' makes… When we started exposing the gangster activities and lifestyles of the 'Brigadiers of Bling'—Jim Gray, Johnny Adair, the Shoukris—we were pilloried by this paramilitary organisation. But, eventually, we were vindicated in exposing the criminals we labelled the paraMafia. And, incredibly—if not inevitably—that vindication came from within the UDA itself.

And from the very top down.

In short, instead of abusing the media, as they had in the past with, for example, their attempted 'boycotts' of us, they began to use media contacts. In a complete *volte face* the mainstream UDA now began to brief *us!* They began to leak documents to us aimed not only at undermining and vilifying 'The Mummy's Boys' and their mob, but also aimed at shafting anyone who still supported them, like the rebel South-East Antrim Brigade headed up by Gary Fisher and Tommy 'Millions' Kirkham.

And the fact that Jim Gray had wanted me dead was confirmed once and for all: by no less a personage than another

UDA brigadier, the man who took over from both the Shoukris in North Belfast. And he told Hugh Jordan, a friend and *Sunday World* colleague of mine: 'Jim Gray wanted Jim McDowell shot dead…' I have since found out that he even took his death wish on me to Inner-Council level. But the Inner Council vetoed his request.

I have my own theories about their reason for doing so. A primary reason was that Jackie McDonald, even then, was trying to take the organisation to 'another place'. And he definitely didn't want loyalists lumbered with the murder of another journalist, like the LVF murder of Martin O'Hagan, or the 'heat' that would come on the UDA from the police if that happened.

I also have no doubt Gray went to his grave in Roselawn Cemetery alongside his son, Jonathan, whose life he had ruined, still wishing I was buried six feet down in that same graveyard.

After the Shoukris were deposed—and, of course, the *Sunday World* had been right exposing them as gangsters all along, more loyal, as they say in Belfast, to the old unit of currency known as the 'half crown', than the Crown—a UDA veteran I had known since I first started as a cub reporter in the *Belfast News Letter,* passed me some information. His name was Sammy Duddy.

Now, down the years, the late Mr Duddy and I hadn't exactly been buddies. He knew my views on paramilitaries, the pariahs of our society. But to be fair to him, he became one of the pioneers of the UDA moving away from the clichéd 'violence of the past', and he played an integral, influential and crucial role in getting rid of the gangsters in UDA ranks: and at quite a considerable cost, not least to his personal safety and that of his family. A quirky detail about Sammy is that he became a key adviser to the UDA—in spite of having been a Danny-La-Rue-style drag artist!

Sammy was one of the first to spurn and turn against the Shoukris, and then to take on the South-East Antrim Brigade for sheltering Ihab and his criminal cronies: even though Duddy lived in the heart of the Rathcoole housing estate which, as I've already explained, was the UDA's operational HQ. And it was he who spilled the beans to me about the day Andre Shoukri made that menacing 'Stop telling lies about me' mobile phone call in the Morning Star bar.

Sammy Duddy told me Shoukri was in the former loyalist prisoners' aid centre on Belfast's York Road, just round the corner from the famous Tiger's Bay UDA mural.

He recalled: 'He was high on drugs. That Nubain stuff. It can make them very aggressive. I was in the prisoners' aid centre. Shoukri was demanding your mobile phone number from me. I told him I didn't have it.'

In fact, Sammy Duddy did have my mobile number at that stage. But he feared a double-cross: if he admitted to Shoukri he had my number, then Shoukri, highly agitated and hyper, would have turned on him and accused him of feeding me, and the *Sunday World*, the 'inside' stories we were running.

Sammy Duddy continued: 'He (Andre) then demanded I ring your office and get your mobile. He knew he couldn't do that himself, because no one would give it to him. So I rang. I told them I needed to speak to you about a story that had appeared.' Duddy would sometimes phone to complain about stories he and the UDA believed to be inaccurate, so he was given my mobile number in good faith.

But with Shoukri in such menacing form, and no doubt surrounded by his tight coterie of Tommy Cousins and the rump of the gang expelled from the UDA, he got my mobile number.

There followed the phone call to me in the Morning Star which ended in such farce.

But the information that was eventually to come from the heart of the mainstream UDA was to be even more explosive. In essence, these were secret files detailing the activities of the SEA Brigade and the Shoukris, the result of internal UDA investigations, and part of Jackie McDonald's attempts to clean up the organisation, the contents of which were pure dynamite.

Not that the 'mainstream' UDA or the Inner Council who headed up the organisation were lily white or squeaky clean themselves. After all, the 'main man' on the Inner Council, South Belfast Brigadier Jackie McDonald, had once served eight years in jail himself for extortion, the polite term for running a protection racket. And the whole organisation had been steeped in the rackets for over three decades.

Especially pernicious was its prostitution of its own communities: the loan-sharking operations which fleeced their own, Protestant working-class people by lending them money at sky-high interest rates. And how did they ensure these people, many living on or below the poverty line, paid back their loans? They confiscated their benefits books on a weekly basis, making sure that when the poor folk—many of them single mothers trying to bring up kids on their own—got their money from the government, the UDA loansharks were there to get their share.

Still, I had reason to meet McDonald on a number of occasions. And although I made it clear I disagreed vehemently with the UDA's past, and its present, I realised that here was someone trying to mould it around a new future. Of course, we didn't exactly share a pint in the pub, but I remember one aside after a certain occasion when he quipped: 'McDowell, you know, I could like you as a man if it wasn't for that paper you run.'

To which I replied: 'Jackie, you know, I could like you as a man if it wasn't for that organisation you run…'

Yes, just like with David Ervine, sometimes it could be

upfront and personal with Jackie McDonald. But when he decided to rid the UDA of the blight of the 'Brigadiers of Bling', there was nothing personal about it. It was ruthlessly professional, just as it was when he moved against the Shoukris and their mob. Plus, McDonald and his close advisors had learned from the Provos and Sinn Féin in one very important aspect: the value of propaganda.

The secret dossiers which we were to be shown were damning internal documents, including a three-month investigation of the Shoukris' freelance rackets and trousering of the proceeds. Or, in Andre Shoukri's case, punting almost a million quid over the counters of betting shops to earn him the *Sunday World* soubriquet of 'The Bookies' Brigadier'.

The method for getting the documents to us was straightforward. A senior source had been designated by the Inner Council to 'drop' us the stuff. He would phone when the documents were ready. A rendezvous would be arranged with either myself, Hugh Jordan, or both of us. The source would meet us as we sat in a car at the pre-arranged dropping point. Sometimes, the source would get in the vehicle. Most times, he just handed us the stuff and walked on.

And once, to our obvious surprise, he was even accompanied by a brigadier. We got the message then: this was to 'authenticate' that the stuff we were getting was coming from and was sanctioned by top echelons of the Inner Council. For the hard-working staff of the *Sunday World*, who had campaigned so hard against the 'Brigadiers of Bling', here was the hard evidence and from inside the UDA at that.

It goes without saying that the *Sunday World* rigorously checked and followed up all information we received. We have many, many sources and we are not in the business of taking anything at face value—especially when it comes from a terrorist/gangster organisation. We do our own investigations. We don't just swallow propaganda from anyone.

We had already been doing our own 'research' on Tommy 'Millions' Kirkham and the South-East Antrim Brigade, over many years.

We knew all about their drug-dealing. We knew where they had accumulated their property portfolios, their flash cars, and their other ill-gotten and criminal gains. So we did a wee bit more 'research', and we found out that Brigadier Fisher had been running a huge drug-running operation using the cross-Channel and continental haulage business as 'cover': just like the LVF, in fact.

We even took pictures of the private housing complex where the secretive and reclusive Fisher—we still haven't been able to get a picture of him—owned three smart houses.

And we photographed the UDA's HQ in the heart of the massive loyalist housing estate of Rathcoole, on the northern shores of Belfast Lough. South-East Antrim UDA members knew that as the Eastway social club, but what most of them didn't know was that, behind their backs, Fisher and Kirkham were partners in a private land deal involving a plot of land adjacent to the Eastway club.

At least, they were ignorant of that fact until we put them right by printing the story, with pictures, in the *Sunday World*.

The same Eastway Social Club was to loom large in the leaked files we were getting from our source, too. One of those files even showed that 'disaffected' veterans within the breakaway South-East Antrim Brigade ranks were rebelling against their own 'rebel' leadership. But, importantly, this stuff that our senior source within the mainstream UDA was feeding us 'stood up' 'propaganda', or not.

One file was headed: CRIMES AGAINST THE COMMUNITY: SOUTH-EAST ANTRIM. It was described by those probing both the Shoukris and the SEA Brigade 'Dirty Dozen' as an 'overview' from 'grassroots' members of the SEA 'opposed to criminality'. The file said that veterans in the SEA UDA 'are not happy at their own leadership for permitting Ihab and Yuk Shoukri and Alan McClean to attend their Brigade meetings'. (Andre Shoukri was behind bars at this stage.)

It added: 'The SEA grassroots membership [say they] resent their Brigade Staff's [the Dirty Dozen's] decision to back a criminal element in north Belfast against the Inner Council.'

The information the mainstream UDA investigators were obviously gathering from within SEA-Brigade ranks indicated, according to this leaked document, that 'Tommy Cousins and Ihab Shoukri (both expelled from the UDA) are frequent visitors to the Eastway social club.' It said that veterans in SEA had 'openly challenged their Brigade Staff over its decision to allow this to take place.'

The file claimed that 'another bone of contention' was the SEA Brigade's decision to allow Ihab Shoukri to live in Islandmagee, in SEA territory. In a full-frontal propaganda blitz on the 'Dirty Dozen', the document passed to us accused them of:

EXTORTION: 'Recently, five senior figures in the SEA have been charged over extortion rackets in the area.'
DRUGS: 'The SEA Brigade Staff are all drug-users and drug-dealers. It is our view that these men are not fit to be in senior positions.'
MURDER: 'One of them (on the Brigade staff) is guilty of the brutal murder of Nelson, who was employed as a door-man at the Chimney Corner Hotel. This man was murdered simply because he had the audacity to challenge these people over drug abuse in the hotel.'

(For the record, but not included in the UDA dossier, Stephen Nelson, also known as 'Raz', was a decent, honourable, brave man. He once worked for the Ulster commercial radio station, Downtown, in the days when they ran discos in pubs, clubs and hotels. They eventually ended that. But big 'Raz' kept the contacts with some places going.

He was running a disco in the Chimney Corner Hotel at weekends. South-East Antrim bogeys wanted to sell drugs in there and he told them to get out. They took off and reported to a 'Commander' based in the Rathcoole housing estate, just a couple of miles away from the Chimney Corner. He in turn led a team which ambushed Stephen Nelson when he finished work that night. They gave him a savage beating. The big lad lay in a coma, his head horrifically swollen to the size of two footballs, according to friends allowed to visit him, before, weeks later, he succumbed to his injuries and died.

At one meeting with our UDA contact, we were given the name of the 'Commander' who sanctioned the murder and led the killer gang. He is one of two brothers who deal dope in Rathcoole. We wrote the story then, but we couldn't name him for legal reasons. I still can't here. He is still walking the streets a free man, in spite of information we received that at one stage, cops had raided his home and discovered that cannabis was being grown there. Another tout—or what?

But back to the file, and its next category, which was:

ARSON: The 'Dirty Dozen' had ordered a bar in the SEA Brigade area to be torched—'petrol was poured on the roof and set alight'—so that punters drinking there would be forced to use the Eastway social club bar instead.

A building close to the same social club had been targeted frequently because it was blocking a development plan masterminded by Fisher and Kirkham. 'On one occasion Fisher ordered UDA personnel to drive a car at the building and set it alight,' the document said.

A business had been 'robbed, attacked and burned' in order to 'embarrass other senior figures within the organisation' after, at Inner-Council level, a crackdown had been ordered on protection rackets.

This particular document ended by claiming that any UDA men still loyal to the mainstream faction and 'bold enough to challenge' the 'Dirty Dozen' ran the risk of being branded touts, being beaten up, or being put out of their homes. The file finally noted: 'This has already been done against a number of people brave enough to speak out.'

At one stage, we were given sight of a document which delivered a damning indictment on the Shoukri brothers. We were led to believe it had been drawn up 'at the highest level': by a Brigadier. And it bluntly stated that:

— Two of the three Shoukri brothers, Andre and Ihab, would have been 'criminals' in 'any walk of life'. And it bluntly stated that the UDA should have kicked them out earlier.
— That the Shoukris 'unfortunately used the UDA to mask over the death, misery and destruction they caused to all the people of Belfast and further afield'.
— Scathingly, that 'the entire structure of the UDA was manipulated and maligned by these so-called "Brigadiers of Bling"'. (Referring to the *Sunday World*'s labelling of Gray, Adair and the Shoukris).
— In the Brigadier's own hand, the Shoukris were accused of running 'drug, vice trade and racketeering' operations, 'starving the loyalist community of its future'.

— That in North Belfast, 'the drugs trade was enormous
and the [protection] rackets were bringing in a large
amount of money'. And the dossier hammered Andre
Shoukri: 'People from the community saw Andre losing
100,000s of pounds [sic] while bullying and blackmailing hard-working local businessmen into closing.'

This catalogue of crime, the document claimed, had driven the
loyalist people of North Belfast 'to breaking point.' It quoted
veteran UDA men in that area as asking, 'Is this what we fought
for, and others, our friends, died for?'

After all of the above, the Brigadier's conclusion hardly came
as a surprise. 'The UDA had no option but to move against
Shoukri' and his mob. The reason? According to that Inner-
Council source: 'They were guilty of dragging the organisation
into disrepute.' Now, how long had the *Sunday World* been
telling the UDA—and the decent people of Ulster—exactly
that?

Another file which came into our possession gave a revealing
insight into double-dealings and double-crosses—and the fear
of them—inside the Shoukri mob. The file focused on John
Boreland, Andre Shoukri's main 'enforcer', eventually jailed for
nine years with Andre on the pub extortion rap.

Nicknamed 'Bonzer' from his days at the Boys' Model School
in Belfast, he's a former Irish League footballer, but he was
playing a very different ballgame inside the Shoukri gang. UDA
investigators had discovered even before he went behind bars
that 'Bonzer' was running a brothel for the Shoukris. And that's
where he 'scored' on them, big time. The file reports: 'Boreland
was entrusted with the revenue from the brothel and other
legal expenses. This money was put away as a secret "nest egg"
by the gang.'

However, the UDA believe that no one except Boreland knew where that cash was stashed. Their file contends that Boreland intended to use that hard-cash cache as insurance, in case, to use the UDA's pithy street patois, the Shoukris were to 'dirty dick' him. That particular dossier also claimed that the mainstream UDA's 'own sources'—in other words, their own prisoners— had heard that 'Bonzer' had 'several hundred thousand pounds' squirreled away in a bunker on the slopes of Carr's Glen, a ravine on the mountain that backdrops the Ballysillan area. It also claimed that Boreland had an arms dump hidden up there. The file stated: 'He thinks he is safe in the knowledge that no one—not even his own family—has any idea where the money and weapons are stashed. He believes he has simply to sit it out until the "heat" blows over when he can dig up the dough and escape to a safe haven'.

Still, the UDA showed it did have a sense of humour—however squint-eyed—when it came to the allegedly hidden weapons. Its internal probe squad reported that 'During the past months, some of the Shoukri supporters who were exiled and are not in jail have made secret visits back to Ballysillan in vain attempts to locate the "hide"'. The file records that local folk reported seeing 'hooded men with metal detectors' on the slopes of Carr's Glen in the dead of night. One resident told them: 'It was like the gold rush to the Klondike for a while up on that Glen…'

For the record, the UDA files eventually proved one story the *Sunday World* had been writing about 'The Mummy's Boys' for years, and that was that the Shoukris couldn't 'keep mum'. In other words, they had to talk. They were touts. These dynamite UDA internal dossiers came our way with the proof we needed. Because of a saga of bungled crimes—among them bank robberies and attempted Tiger kidnappings—plotted by the

North Belfast Brigade with the Shoukris in charge, '24 UDA prisoners are in Maghaberry as a result'.

The implication is clear that it was 'only the ones at the top who knew about these "operations"'. It named them in black and white as Andre and Ihab Shoukri and their main 'brains' in the outfit, Alan 'Nookie Brown' McClean. Significantly, the file which came into our possession stated: 'Suspicion fell on the two Shoukris when men started being caught in these police "stings"'.

And then came the clincher from the Inner Council of the UDA itself. A one-liner: 'We suspect they [the Shoukris] have been informing for the Branch [Special Branch] over a period of 8–9 years.'

That, effectively, spelt the beginning of the end for the Shoukris—and heralded the biggest split ever in the ranks of the Ulster Defence Association. And it proved, once and for all, that, in spite of what we had been subjected to by the Mummy's Boys, we at the *Sunday World* had been proved right.

PART III
'WATCH YOUR BACK'

15 | HARD EVIDENCE

It was a sharp day, the wind scything into us with the cutting edge of the teeth of Cúchulainn, the Hound of Ulster. It was the start of another Irish winter in October 2004 and I had come with a few friends to watch another breed of hound, greyhounds.

I was standing in a field outside the seaside town of Balbriggan, half-way between Newry and Dublin. The Irish Sea was sparkling in the background under a bright sun in a sky as blue as the noses on some of the characters gathered here. Those blue noses were not just a legacy of a lifetime on the booze: a waspish wind sweeping in off the sea delivered a sting which, even before the day's proceedings were started by the expert 'slippers', had many reaching for their hip flasks.

I was doing something that my wife, Lindy, a journalist with the *Belfast Telegraph* for twenty-six years, said I shouldn't be doing. I was about to watch greyhounds chase hares up a field at a coursing meeting. Coursing is banned in the North, as it is in the rest of the UK.

I'd never been before, so I went for two reasons: as a reporter, to make a judgment on the 'sport' first-hand and to have a jar and a day out. To be honest, the 'sport' I found boring, but not 'barbaric', as claimed by those opposed to it. The greyhounds were muzzled, so no hares could be damaged—and they are beautiful animals, especially on the move: no human, not even gold-medal-winning Olympic sprinters, can match the magic of the sleek speed and motion of a hare in full flight. And as for fright? I didn't see any hares die of a heart attack. And surely they have that inherent speed and quicksilver, gyrating guile to allow them to escape predators in the wild, or whatever is left of that in Ireland.

I was bored because I don't punt, so I wasn't sucked into the (notional) romance of trying to 'beat the bookies' who had put up their pitches in the field to ply their precarious trade. So I straggled off at a break in the proceedings and found a warm pub with a blazing turf fire.

A few other 'refugees', who had taken the hint from the hares and 'done a runner' too, found me. We remained there until the coursing, accompanied by the cussing of those whose pockets the bookies had picked, had run its course. My mates from 'up the way' joined us. There was a teetotaller in our company, but he was a dyed-in-the-wool Belfast 'doggie man' who, while he didn't imbibe, was there for both the betting and the banter among the coursing fraternity drawn from throughout the four provinces.

In this pub after the coursing, chemists rubbed shoulders with coalmen, farmers bartered over the price of a winning greyhound with financiers, and bankers roiled over the day's racing with bread delivery men. And pints were slung faster than dockers slinging sacks in the hold of a cement boat.

It was what I would class as a 'wheeker' day out. Not right up there with the day the dear oul' Ulster rugby team won the European Cup at Lansdowne Road at the end of another winter month, January 1999: the day with that huge invasion of

Dublin by an (apolitical) rugby army when we truly united Ireland. We turned the country then into a 32-County Ulster!!! And the day didn't end at that pub with the blazing turf fire a few miles outside Balbriggan. The 'Aughnacloys', the boys, I was with had met some coursing compadres from Newry. So on our way back over the border, we decided to re-rendezvous in a magnificent pub in the border town, The Bridge, then owned by my friends of many years, Michael and Bernie Toner.

To say they had made their business 'blossom' in this beauty of a bar stands up to literal scrutiny: for their floral displays, all around the pub, and even up on the flat roof overlooking the road, were legendary. Bernie and Michael took great pride in their flowers. They also took great pride in their bar being dubbed— by me—in print, 'The Peace Pub'. Right throughout the Troubles, in spite of the many atrocities committed in and around the city of Newry, any hint of trouble was taboo in The Bridge. Indeed, the proud record of the proprietors before they sold it two years ago was that, in over forty years of running The Bridge, they had never had to bar one person because of a barney.

We hadn't been there long with our acquaintances from Newry when my mobile rang. Unusually for me, I'd only taken half a dozen calls that Sunday. Usually, it's many more: the calls a consequence of whatever had appeared in the paper that morning. I had parried the calls, telling some where I was and saying I'd talk to, or meet them, on the Monday. I couldn't parry this one. It was Lindy. And it wasn't to complain about me being at the coursing.

Instead, it was an urgent summons home.

'There are people in the house to see you. They've told me not to talk too much over this phone. But I need you to get home as quickly as possible,' Lindy said.

Fearing the worst, I asked if anything had happened to any-one belonging to me.

'No,' Lindy replied. 'But you need to come home as quickly as possible.'

'I'll be home in no more than an hour,' I assured her.

That was one pint that wasn't finished. I told the lads with me what was happening. They didn't finish their drinks either. We got into the car with the (teetotal) driver at the wheel and, sinking the gutty in a big Merc, he had me home in forty-eight minutes. I know. I was counting.

The friends I was with were concerned. They wanted to come into the house with me in case Lindy had been making that phone call under duress: in other words, they feared that my family could be being held hostage by gunmen waiting to shoot me.

But when I saw the cars outside our front door I knew who it was. I told the boys it was all right, to go on and I'd phone them later.

When I got into the house, there was a virtual posse waiting. The 'reception committee' waiting in the kitchen of our house —already fortified like a police station with bullet-resistant windows, security lights on every corner and at the front door, TV monitors in most rooms, and a 'Hawkeye' instant-response alarm supplied by the PSNI to be carried into every room in case of terrorist attack—was impressive.

But they weren't there to arrest me.

Sitting around our kitchen table was one person I am prepared to name: Hugh Jordan, my colleague in the *Sunday World*, and two other people, whom I am not prepared to name. I have to keep their names secret, because, even now, they could be subject to revenge from the terror gang behind this plot.

And, as I have hinted earlier, it was a threat of the worst possible kind. Not to me, but to a member of my family. One of my two sons, Jamie. He was twenty-one at the time and studying for a politics degree at the University of Ulster at

Jordanstown. With a wee car on the road and living with a couple of mates in a house in what we considered a 'safe' area (off the stockbroker-belt Malone Road in Belfast), he was working in a pub two or three nights a week to put money in his pocket and to put petrol in the tank.

The two contacts sitting in my kitchen revealed that the LVF had discovered that Jamie was doing bartending shifts in an upmarket pub/club on the leafy Lisburn Road in swish south Belfast. And they revealed that this gang was plotting to kidnap Jamie and do serious harm to him: or worse, kill him.

Jamie had been off work and out with his mates in a bar that Sunday night. But by the time I hit the house, his mother had already phoned him and got him home.

These two contacts had an 'informant' from whom they'd picked up the intelligence about Jamie. The informant told them about the threat, made by an LVF gang based in north Belfast and Antrim town. This gang dealt in drugs, taking in consignments being shipped into Ulster from across the water in England, from the Continent—mainly from the Gary 'Mammy's Boy' Marno mob in Spain—from Amsterdam, or from the major drug gangs in Dublin and Limerick; when these gangsters weren't too busy knocking each other off in gangland feuds, that is.

This gang was run by two brothers: their father was a well-known loyalist, called Laurence Kincaid. And, a vain man, when he had two sons to two different women: well, that vanity dictated that he call BOTH of them Laurence, too! Both Laurences headed up the North Belfast/Antrim LVF drugs gang, but the brother based in Antrim town clung on to the moniker Laurence, and the one based in North Belfast went by the nickname 'Duffer'. He is a convicted drug dealer. We even ran a picture of him on a boating trip while he was supposed to be serving his sentence. That, literally, whipped up a wave of outrage And it undoubtedly contributed to the Kincaids' hatred of the *Sunday World* and of me. The contacts said the LVF plotted this to get back at me, as Editor of the *Sunday World*, for running a consistent campaign exposing their evil poisoning of young people through drugs.

What the LVF had planned to do, as told to me, Lindy and Jamie by the very reliable contacts in my home that Sunday night, was target Jamie as he left the bar, which was usually in the wee small hours of the morning after the customers had left and the bar was cleared up, ready for business the next morning. 'They're planning at the very least to attack Jamie— possibly to beat him up or shoot him in the legs—and then plant a large quantity of drugs on him,' we were told.

I asked why.

'Because they believe that will be them getting their own back on you,' the contact said. 'One of them was overheard saying: "How would big McDowell like it if the peelers find his son like this—and he ends up banged up in jail on a drugs bust".'

Bad enough. But there was worse to follow. 'Hold on. That's not all. At least one of the gang—and we're not sure which one—is also talking about "taking Jamie out". Killing him. Shooting him dead with a shotgun which can't be traced,' the contact finished.

Now, this was hard—very hard—to take in. We'd lived for a long time by this stage with many threats, both formal and informal, but they had always been focused outside my home. Now there was one being brought home to us. And it wasn't directed at me this time.

Plus, there was another terrifying twist.

We asked how the gang had found out where Jamie was working—the bohemian Lisburn Road with its bistros, bars and pavement cafés is a gulf the size of the Grand Canyon away from their shebeens and drugs dens in the Ballysillan housing estate in the shadow of Belfast's Black Mountain. My contacts named a man—who I still can't name here for legal reasons, much as I'd like to—who they said was dealing in drugs for the LVF. The gang were 'leaning on' him to set Jamie up, we were told.

Jamie, listening to this, was incredulous. 'He's one of my friends,' he stated, disbelief pulsing through his voice. 'But he wouldn't be working for the LVF,' Jamie stated. 'I even think he's a Catholic.'

The contact was adamant. 'Jamie, son,' he told him, looking him straight in the eye, 'believe me: this is who is setting you up.'

But there was another jolt for us: our contacts told us that the LVF didn't only know where Jamie worked part-time in the pub/club: they had traced his movements to and from the Jordanstown campus of the University of Ulster to the north of Belfast—close to where 'Duffer' Kincaid had his family home at the time. (Kincaid owned and used other houses for his drug-dealing operations: he and his LVF cohorts even dug out bunkers in the back gardens of houses in Ballysillan, where they hoarded their drugs and even had tunnels linking them. Those tunnels were meant to act as 'rat runs', or escape routes, in the event of Drugs Squad raids. They were also intended as underground evacuation routes for use during the many feuds which erupted between the Ulster Volunteer Force and the breakaway LVF founded by Billy 'King Rat' Wright. When we discovered this network of tunnels, we ran a front page headlining Kincaid's mob as the 'Tunnel Rats'.) The contacts also told us that the LVF had the make and registration number of the wee Nissan Micra car Jamie was driving at the time to get him to and from university.

Absorbing this information, we thanked the contacts, sincerely, for the possibly life-saving information, shocking as it was. They left our home in the early hours.

We had to take action, quickly. That night, late as it was, we checked the Internet for flights out of the country the next day. We found some going to Spain. And far away from Marbella, the hangout of a team of exiled Ulster drug-dealers with strong links to the loyalist paraMafia.

We were looking for two seats: if our son had to get out of the country, we didn't want him going on his own. We contacted a good mate of his the next morning and filled the lad in on the previous night's briefing. We told him Jamie was getting offside for a couple of weeks, to try to take the heat off the threat to him and we needed someone to go to Spain with him.

In spite of both boys missing out on their university studies— Jamie eventually had to scrub a whole term—this friend agreed to go with Jamie without hesitation. We will be eternally grateful to that lad and to his family for their support at that time.

Both boys flew out the next day. They were away for a couple of weeks. That gave us breathing space to act and act quickly. That same day, I went to the police station at Ladas Drive in east Belfast, which covers the area where I live.

My address is no secret, to terrorists or to anyone else. Both Lindy and I are journalists, and we need people to talk to us to get our stories, so we have always been in the phone book and been open about where we live.

The detectives at Ladas Drive—the old HQ of the Special Branch and formerly known as the Castlereagh Holding Centre, where terrorist suspects were interrogated—knew all about my home. It was from Castlereagh that the original order had gone out that a 'Hawkeye' instant response alarm system should be installed in our house. Plus, the police there would ensure that their mobile patrols, especially during the night, kept a special watch on our house. In particular a smashing big fellow, now retired from the PSNI, called George McAllister, was our 'guardian angel', though he would baulk at the title.

Big George was away somewhere on duty, but two detectives came down to see me. I told them what had happened. I asked that they check their own sources—the paramilitaries were, and still are, riddled with police touts—to get us any more information and to take appropriate action if the North Belfast LVF were planning to harm, or kill, our son.

That morning I had prepared a special statement myself, setting out in precise detail what we had been told by the 'contacts' the night before. After I left the police station, I went to a lawyer friend, Ted Jones, at his office in downtown Belfast. I told him, in confidence, who the 'contacts' were in my house with Hugh Jordan the night before.

Ted listened intently. He knew Hugh Jordan, and, with his encyclopaedic knowledge of 'the street' in Ulster—he knows both politics, and paramilitaries, inside out—he also knew both 'contacts'. He agreed that their advice had to be taken very seriously indeed.

I asked him to accept into his safekeeping the statement I had typed up earlier that morning, which now included the visit to Castlereagh to see the two detectives. I told Ted: 'I want you to have this. If anything happens to Jamie, to me, or to anybody else in my family on foot of what we were told last night, I want people to know I did everything possible, within the law, to try to prevent it and blow the whistle on those planning it.'

Ted agreed to hold the document for me, saying that he hoped Jamie would be OK, and told me to watch everyone in the family.

The two detectives at Castlereagh had obviously been checking their sources. The next day, uniformed officers arrived at my door. They wanted me to sign a police warning message. This message was entitled: 'POLICE MESSAGE—CASTLEREAGH DCU [District Command Unit], CMC Ref No. 04/55.'

I have received countless warning messages, but this time it was different. This time, the message was not addressed to me: chillingly, it was addressed to 'SON OF JIM MCDOWELL'. The message came as a slap in the face to both Lindy and myself. Although we had no doubts about the truth of what we had been told in our own house by the 'contacts' two nights previously, the message coldly stated in bold, black capital letters:

'POLICE HAVE RECEIVED INFORMATION THAT MEMBERS OF LVF INTEND TO CARRY OUT AN ATTACK ON A PERSON BELIEVED TO BE THE SON OF JIM MCDOWELL EDITOR OF THE *SUNDAY WORLD*. THIS ATTACK MAY BE RELATED TO HIS EMPLOYMENT.'

That final line confirmed that Jamie was being set up in the pub/club where he had been working part-time.

The police never give further details of the stark information on the forms in case it compromises their own sources, their 'touts' in other words. You are just handed the warning forms (they are carbon copies) by a uniformed officer, who almost certainly knows nothing about the background, you sign the top copy, and you get to keep one. That's it. As bland and blunt as that. And sometimes, that can be bloody frustrating and infuriating.

We were glad we had got our Jamie out of the country. It may have disrupted his studies at the University of Ulster but at least it saved his life. As Lindy recalls:

'Living with threats over the years we were never so naïve as to think our family might be immune to danger. Even members of our wider family have been verbally abused because of Jim's role with the *Sunday World*.

'But it goes without saying that the shock of a direct threat to murder one of your children is hard to come to terms with. Our boys have grown up with an awareness that their dad's life was under threat and that security precautions were a necessary part of everyday life. As Jim points out elsewhere in this book, we're well aware that we're not the only family who've had to live like this. It's not so much that you get used to it but you do learn to cope with it.

'For the boys it hasn't been easy. The first really serious threats to Jim's life I remember, date back to the time when Jamie was in his very early teens. Every day when I was in work he used to ring me from school at break-time and then at dinner time with the same questions, "Is Dad still OK? Are you sure he's all right?"

'Sometimes the question was just the blunt, "Is Dad still alive?" You don't need to be a psychologist to know that isn't good for a child.

'It affected so many aspects of their lives. Simple things—like we couldn't allow them to sleep over regularly in friends' houses the way kids want to. Why not? Simple reason—we'd have to reciprocate. And we just couldn't take the risk of having kids to stay if there was a chance of any kind of attack on our house. That's not to say we didn't occasionally have kids to stay, but only at time when we were confident (with police assurances) that the threat was very low.

'Talking to people about the threats was difficult too. You felt you were being melodramatic. I often got the feeling people were thinking, "What sort of nutter is this woman?"

'You have to try to rationalise. To remember that police intelligence comes from a variety of sources and that some threats may be less potent or serious than others. But you'd be a fool not to treat any sort of death threat with some degree of seriousness.

'And the sheer scale of the threats that Jim has had over the years—we could easily paper the walls of the downstairs loo with all those warning forms—was alarming to put it mildly. It has to say something about him that he's collected death threats from every single paramilitary outfit in Northern Ireland. Not to mention assorted drug gangs...

'The other side, though, is the response from decent people who live in areas controlled by the terror gangsters. Time and time again I've watched as Jim has been approached by strangers who've thanked him for what he and the *Sunday World* have been doing. Some of the stories have been shocking in the extreme. Many heart-rending. For obvious reasons we can't reveal details of some of the accounts we've heard. But it all underlines how very important it is that journalists confront what is happening—and expose the criminals behind it.

'I'm proud of what Jim has done over the years in taking them on and I'm proud of our sons Jamie and his brother Micah, for understanding and accepting the constraints that that has placed on their own lives.

'From my own point of view I support Jim one hundred per cent. But I defy anyone not to feel a chill of horror and fear when you look at a form baldly stating that someone's trying to kill your husband. Or, as in the story Jim has just outlined, your son.

'The ultimate irony, of course, is that all these threats have come from outfits which would all, in their own way, style themselves "freedom fighters". So much for their concept of freedom—particularly freedom of speech.'

Jamie himself, who had the balls to come back—in spite of all the threats to his da and others around him (and that direct one to himself) adds:

'I had been sitting in a pub on the Lisburn Road that night, just a few hundred metres down the street from the place where I had been working.

'Having a few pints on a Sunday was pretty much a religious exercise for me, as it still is. It's the first opportunity that people who work in the bar trade generally get to have a drink after the weekend, especially if you work part-time, since it's almost out of the question to have a Friday or Saturday night off.

'So the atmosphere was relaxed and everyone was generally happy to see the back of another long, sweaty working week-end—and the amount of drink being taken mirrored that!

'Most of the early phone calls I had received were from mates who also work in pubs and who had been enquiring if anybody knew where was open for a late drink. Bars shut at midnight on Sundays. And by the time bar staff haul themselves out of bed after finishing up work at maybe four or five in the morning, there isn't much time left to have a drink. That's why some bars would stay open for a 'lock-in' for bar staff.

'When I saw my ma's number come up on my mobile, I thought she was just calling to see how I was, as I was living away from home and hadn't been to my parents' house for a few days.

'But the tone of her voice immediately told me otherwise. She sounded upset but she wouldn't tell me what was wrong over the phone. My first instinct was to ask if my da was OK, as over the years I have tried to prepare myself mentally for hearing that some scum-bag has finally caught up with him.

'But she assured me that everyone was safe and after a few minutes of my relentless questioning she finally told me that the threat involved me… but nothing more.

'Leaving the bar, different scenarios began to race through my head. I wondered if it was to do with something that was going to happen in the future, or whether something was happening now, in the bar where I sat. I didn't once question who would want to harm me. I had no idea who it was, but I immediately knew why.

I had taken small amounts of grief before about my da, the odd aside or comment while working in the bar or the odd smart-arse trying to be funny, but nothing to lose sleep over. I have always figured that if he is pissing off a drugs dealer or a paramilitary enough for them to have a go at me, then he must be doing something right.

'There have been threats that he has received in the past that have been directed at "Jim McDowell and his family", where my da had taken me or my brother Micah for a pint and explained that we have to keep an eye over our shoulder and what to do if the house comes under attack and so on. I had, however, never had a threat made against myself individually.

'I made my way home to find my mother sitting at a table full of grim-looking faces with all eyes pinned on me. The intensity of the atmosphere in that room was overpowering. Sobering (in every sense) is not the word!

'I immediately recognised one of the people who had taken the evidence to my parents' house. I had met the man a few times before and was glad to see his face, but it also sent a chill up my spine to know that the situation was serious enough for him to be there at this time of night.

'I sat down and they explained what was happening. Initially I felt disbelief and tried to argue otherwise when one of the contacts mentioned the name of a person involved in the threat against me. But as they explained what they knew, the dots began to join up.

'I'd always thought of the guy in question as a bit of a nosy boy. He was always asking about where I was living, what shifts I was working, what days I went to university, when and where I was going out. I just put it down to him being the inquisitive type though. You don't assume that somebody who's generally pleasant and friendly is actually asking questions in order to set you up.

'You might think, reading what I am saying, that overall this would have been a frightening experience—and it was—to a certain degree. But fear was not what I was feeling most, not out of bravado or machismo, but because growing up I had got used to the threats and resigned myself to the fact that if they were going to attack my parents' home, well, they would inevitably be attacking me, my mother and my brother as well.

I was really pissed off and angry. And the time I had to spend in Spain when my parents arranged for me and a friend to get out of the country made me even more angry. But now, when I look back on it, I just think how lucky I was —and how grateful I am to those who warned me of what was going to happen.'

The threat eventually faded, but that wasn't the last we were to hear of Duffer Kincaid. And, in contrast to what was planned by his LVF gang for our Jamie, it was Duffer himself who ended up shot.

That happened in the early hours of the morning of Sunday 7 August 2005. Convicted drug-dealer Kincaid was shot in the shoulder as he and another man attacked a house in north Belfast in the pre-dawn hours of that Sunday morning.

A vicious internecine loyalist feud—between the Ulster Volunteer Force and Kincaid's LVF—was raging at the time. Just weeks before his August 2005 escapade, the UVF had been blamed for firing ten shots at the house where Kincaid was then living. When Kincaid and his co-accused, William Anderson, first appeared in court in connection with the house attack, a prosecuting barrister linked the assault to that vendetta, and opposed bail for Kincaid, claiming it would lead to further violence.

However, Kincaid eventually did get out on bail. But it still took the case over two years to come to a conclusion. Suddenly at the start of 2008, both Kincaid, then 35, and Anderson, 22, decided that rather than go to trial, they would plead guilty to causing criminal damage to the home of Trevor Dowie, the father-of-three whose family home they had attacked in Glenside Park in north Belfast.

Originally, they'd been charged with attempted intimidation, but now copped a plea to this lesser charge. What Judge Norman Lockie, sitting in the Crown Court in Downpatrick, heard, was that in the attack on the Dowie home, Anderson had hurled a paving slab, stones and bricks through the living room and other windows while Kincaid watched nearby, sitting on a moped.

It was explained to the court that forty-seven-year-old Mr Dowie's home had been attacked before, six months previous to the August 2005 assault, when a gang of men had invaded it. Prosecuting lawyer David Russell told Judge Lockie that, in the later attack, fearing his home was being subjected to the same violence, Dowie had loaded his legally-held Browning pistol, aimed it at Kincaid, and shot him in the left shoulder. Kincaid, wounded and bleeding, sped off. But he collapsed and fell off the moped a short distance away.

The court was told that Trevor Dowie also fired two 'unaimed shots' at Anderson after sighting him in his garden, but missed. Dowie was arrested and charged with the attempted murder of Kincaid, but claimed that, especially after the raid on his house half a year earlier, he was firing in defence of his home and his family. Mr Russell explained that no prosecution had been followed up against Mr Dowie.

Mr Russell said that Kincaid, with an address at Flush Road in Belfast and Anderson, from Rockmount, Comber Road, in Dundonald in the east of the city, were arrested. He said Anderson refused to answer questions. But Kincaid claimed that he was drunk and didn't know what Anderson had planned.

Both walked free from the court, Kincaid getting a nine-month prison sentence suspended for a year, and Anderson having served enough time on remand to justify his immediate release.

Interestingly, before he handed down those sentences, Judge Lockie heard evidence that Kincaid had 'radically altered his lifestyle'. The court was told that he had become chairman of a community housing group and was co-operating with police 'to reduce crime' in the Ballysillan area, which had formerly been his main 'turf' when he was an LVF drugs Godfather.

What a contrast that was to 2004 when Kincaid had appeared in court on drugs charges and a police inspector testified on oath that Duffer was working as a drug-dealer for loyalist paramilitaries. Now, we were being told Kincaid was, in essence, a community worker. Where had I heard that before—sitting face-to-face with Johnny 'Mad Dog' Adair, perhaps, before his licence was revoked because he'd returned to his bad old ways, and he ended up back behind bars?

I found that conversion 'on the road to Damascus' hard to swallow. And I wasn't the only one. The day after the Kincaid and Anderson court case, Trevor Dowie, the family man whose house had been attacked by the LVF not once, but *twice* in six months talked to the *Sunday World*.

Dowie told us how, in February 2005, while he was in hospital, a masked and armed LVF gang stormed into his home. Only his wife Anne and his teenage daughter Kelly were at home. Both were held at gunpoint and threatened with rape as the raiders demanded the keys to Mr Dowie's gun cabinet. Terrified Kelly only escaped being shot in the leg because the gun jammed three times. The gang only fled when the Dowie's guard dogs started barking and security lights flashed on.

Trevor Dowie told our reporter that he still believes Duffer's LVF mob was behind that brutal raid. And he emphasised that he has no affiliation to any paramilitary group and that his shooting of Duffer had nothing to do with any loyalist feud. That, at least,

backs up what was said in court in Downpatrick when Judge
Lockie was told that it was now believed, in spite of what was said
at the original remand hearing, that the attack on the Dowie
home in August 2005 was not part of such a vendetta.

Trevor Dowie told us, 'Duffer was shot because he targeted
my family and he targeted us because I had something he
wanted: guns. It's as simple as that.'

Talking the day after Kincaid walked free from court—the very
same LVF gangster we have believed all along is a police tout—
Trevor Dowie made it quite clear to us that he doesn't, believe
Laurence 'Duffer' Kincaid has 'radically altered his lifestyle.'

That Sunday 2 March 2008, we blew up a mugshot of Mr
Dowie and put it opposite a similar mugshot of Kincaid on the
front page. Above both head-and-shoulder pictures we ran a
'double-deck', or two-line, headline in capital letters which
blasted out:

LVF'S DUFFER WILL KILL ME

DAD WHO SHOT TERROR BOSS SAYS THAT HE'LL BE MURDERED
BY GANG.

THIS is the man who legally shot LVF godfather Duffer
Kincaid—and LIVED to tell the tale to the *Sunday World*.
But now brave Trevor Dowie, left, believes his life may end
at the age of 47 years. Because convicted drugs dealer
Kincaid, 35, walked FREE from court this week after cop-
ping a plea for his part in an attack on the Dowie family
home. In a previous attack, members of Duffer's drug-
dealing gang had threatened to RAPE Mr Dowie's wife and
daughter. But now, the courageous father-of-three says he's
a dead man walking. In an exclusive interview he told us:
'My biggest fear is that Duffer will get his mates to come
after me, to kill me. He will get them to do his dirty work
for them. This is far from over.'

16 | 'I'M GOING TO SHOOT YOU STONE F*****G DEAD!'

The police, both formally and informally, continually drummed into me that I had to change my movements at all times, especially during threats, and even now. The precautions they gave verbally were often doubled up by their little red book detailing safety precautions and given to persons under threat.

Both officially, when I was handed warning forms, and unofficially, by my friends who are policemen when I was having a jar with them, I would get the same well-meaning lecture: 'Change your movements. Change your route into work every morning. Change the times you come in. Change the pubs you drink in. Change your habits: period.'

Practical advice. But bloody impossible to follow. I am what I am, as are most people, a creature of habit. The terrorists know that. That is how they targetted people in the past with accuracy and often, as long as they got their primary homework right, with impunity.

I well remember one of my best friends, Kevin Sheehy, one-time head of the RUC/PSNI Drugs Squad, telling me: 'McDowell, the first thing the terrorists plot is not their attack.

It's their escape.' But it was Kevin who also warned me that my weakest point would be an unguarded moment, like going to the wc in a pub. 'That's when you're most likely to get hit,' he told me, 'when you're standing with your back to the door.'

I tried to keep that in mind. Even though I've now got arthritis in my neck, and not from thirty-seven years in a rugby scrum, mind you, but from standing having a pee with my neck craned round and my head pointing in the opposite direction to where I'm aiming. God only knows how many pairs of boots I've splashed. Not only my own, but punters standing beside me.

Safety advice was to come from many quarters: some of them strange enough, but some of them glaringly obvious, if just a wee bit off-putting. Towards the end of my days playing rugby, I started running marathons. Pockled and hirpled around eleven of them—the ache in my hips and knees now is appropriate punishment for doing so much damage to the pavements of Ulster, not only during the marathons themselves, but blattering in the sixty or seventy miles a week in training as well.

That was during the early eighties, when the police passed on two pieces of vital safety information. The first was to stop going out on training runs from my own home. That was making me too much of an 'open' and slow-moving target for any terrorists who may be stalking me. This meant getting into the car every time I was going out for a run and picking a different start location every day. I'm still doing it.

That's OK in the summer, when only the sweat is drying on you after a run. It's a different matter in the dead of winter in the brittle cold when the sweat and snotters are both freezing and drying on you and you face a drive of up to half an hour or more to get home into a steaming shower.

The second piece of advice was always to take a mobile phone with me when running. The reason? As one 'Golden

Oldie' police sportsman, with almost as many miles on the clock as I had (in every sense!), explained: 'They shoot you, you're not dead, but you're down, and you need help: the mobile is the quickest way to dial 999.'

Lovely, that made training before the scrake of dawn or on dark nights a very inviting prospect indeed. But, again, I took the advice, and took the mobile phone. You never know…

There was one incident which literally stopped me in my tracks. I was fond of using a City-Council leisure centre in south Belfast as my base for going out for a run after I left Lindy into work for her 8 a.m. starts in the *Belfast Telegraph*. It was especially handy a couple of days a week in the winter when the prospect of heading out in the dark, rain and cold was eased by the prospect of an instant warm shower in the leisure centre when a few miles had been pumped in.

I got to know the staff in there very well; they were good people. But one morning, two of the girls stopped me at the door. I'd been away working somewhere out of town for three or four days.

They took me aside. They knew who I was, and the kind of stories we covered in the paper. 'Look, Jim, you haven't been here for the past few days. But the last three days in a row, there's been a car sitting out in the car park with three blokes in it,' one of the centre's staff explained.

'It's been here from just before the time you usually arrive,' explained the other, adding: 'And it's stuck around for about fifteen minutes. The guys in it look very dodgy and furtive. They look edgy, and are always on the lookout.'

'We're just a bit concerned for you,' said the first girl. 'We didn't know whether to call the police. They're not here this morning. We checked. But we thought we should tell you. We're just not happy about it.'

I thanked them. They were going beyond the call of duty, but their diligence could have meant the difference between life and death: *my* life and death. I left the centre, thinking: Is nothing sacrosanct, even going out for a run to get a bloody bubble of sweat on my baldy head?

However, I (discreetly) scouted out the leisure centre car park the next morning around the time I would usually be driving in there. I did that by driving through the nearby parkland, the pathways of which were prohibited to motorists. But it was still dark, there were few pedestrians or dog walkers, so I just stuck on the hazard lights and pretended I was a City-Council Parks employee or official.

I stopped at the top of a hill, behind trees, overlooking the car park. A car was sitting in the sports centre car park. The windows were a bit steamed up: they'd been there a while. But there were three people inside.

I didn't get any closer. No point in handing them anything on a plate if they were looking for me, but I noted the car registration number. I passed it on to a civil servant I knew who could access car registration numbers. I'd used her in the past, in spite of the Data Protection Act, which, in certain circumstances, and especially to hacks like me, is the biggest piece of piss-off legislation ever passed in Parliament. This particular professional, who never accepted payments, had helped out with certain information when we'd been under the cosh before. And she made it clear she would be insulted by the offer of money. She was as anti-paraMafia as we were.

She came back to me within a few hours. The registration number was that of a stolen car. It had probably been stolen for a purpose. To cause me harm: and it would then be torched like so many before it.

The warning from the two kind girls in the leisure centre had been prescient. I took it seriously. I stopped training out of the leisure centre with immediate effect.

———

Another word of warning about my 'personal movements' which I also took very seriously, came from perhaps the strangest source of all. And it is one I have heeded resolutely, if not religiously, since.

There was a certain pub I was fond of sinking a pint in, up an entry, or alleyway. As I've already explained, a lot of the great traditional boozers in Belfast in the past were up entries, and the few remaining still are. I was in there on my own swallowing a sup of stout while waiting to meet a story contact. I didn't really twig to this myself, but there was a man standing at the bar, muscular and very well groomed. I should have copped from the telltale black leather jacket he was wearing that he 'had a past'. Still, he was bothering no one. And I thought I wasn't bothering him.

Every time my mobile rang, because of the poor signal inside, I would tell the caller to 'hang on' and I would walk out-side and up the entry to a side street where the mobile would work. I must have done this about five times in the hour I was in there on this particular occasion.

When I was leaving, the well-groomed guy in the black leather jacket addressed me by name. I thought: Here we go again... never a bloody pint in peace.

But he simply said to me: 'Listen, I know your face from the paper and TV and that. I'm no threat to you. But let me tell you, you're a big threat to yourself.'

I asked him point blank: 'Are you threatening me, boss?'

'No, not at all,' he said. 'But, see, every time that phone of yours rings, you walk outside. Now, I've watched you standing facing the door the whole time you've been in here, keeping an eye on everyone coming in, just in case. That's fair enough. But every time that phone rings, and you walk outside... well, if I wanted to kill you, all I would have to do is get your mobile number, phone you from outside in that entry, and when you walk outside—shoot you dead.'

I thanked him for the observation, and the advice. I offered to buy him a pint. He refused, politely. Said he was just doing me 'a good turn'.

Three days later I met a contact of mine from the Shankill. I described your man in the downtown Belfast bar. He knew him, and told me who he was. I was right about the black leather jacket. He was not long out of jail, a loyalist double killer who had copped a double life sentence but got out early thanks to the Good Friday Agreement.

Now, when my mobile rings inside any pub, my reply is as 'coached' by the double killer. I say, simply: 'McDowell. I'll ring you back in five minutes.' And I give it the full five, at least, before walking outside, checking the entry, or street outside, before putting a bit of distance between myself and the pub and phoning back.

Coincidentally—and he wasn't to know this—that double loyalist killer's prediction was right on the money, but this incident took place at another bar, close by, which shall remain nameless.

As I have pointed out previously, the people who own bars sometimes don't have a say in who drinks in them, especially in some parts of Ulster. A good fella—in fact, a lad I used to play rugby with—has since taken this pub over, has hoovered out the shady clientele, and is now making a smashing success of the pub. However, this incident happened under the old management, one night in the late nineties when I was actually waiting to meet an ex-cop there. And it sparked one of the most immediate threats I was ever to get.

This pub was dimly lit, as becomes one of the oldest pubs in the city, but the scent of the turf burning in a fireplace so huge the iron grate must have been built in a dry dock in the Harland & Wolff shipyard, wasn't the only aroma discernible in the place. I should have been able to smell the drug-dealers way down the back of the paving-stoned seating area of the pub: that class of criminal also has very distinct aroma, a smell which equates closely with that which comes out of a dog's arse.

But in the dim light, I didn't clock the drug-dealers. They did me, however, and a couple of them came up to the bar, where I and a couple of friends had just ordered.

One in particular was about as welcoming as a pitbull in a kindergarten. He didn't talk to me: he snarled, a slobbering tirade of spite and spittle. But I didn't exactly reply with words hewn out of the *Kofi Annan United Nations Pocket Guide to Good Peacekeeping*, either.

The vitriol quickly became more volcanic, then the drugs hoodie erupted. 'I'm away to get a f*****g gun, you baldie b*****d. I'm going to shoot you stone 'f*****g dead,' he exploded, heading for the door.

Now, I didn't know who he was by name. But I certainly knew which drugs team he was connected to: the INLA, otherwise known as the Irish National Liberation Army. This organisation had been decimated many times in the past by internecine feuding, and as I placed on record in *Godfathers*, one of the worst threats I have ever received came from one of their most feared killers, Hugh 'Cueball' Torney: and that came *after* Torney himself had been shot dead in yet another internal vendetta. One of his henchmen came up to me at a boxing match in the Ulster Hall, put his hand out to shake mine, and coolly told me to my face: 'Cueball wants you dead… from the grave!'

I survived that rather direct threat. But this one I wasn't so sure about. The drugs scum who was threatening to get a gun to shoot me dead now was a member of one of the most ruthless INLA drugs gangs. I had reported on one of their previous atrocities in depth, the brutal murder of pub manager Colm Mahon. This happened at a bar-cum-nightclub, Frames, at the back of the *Belfast Telegraph* newspaper HQ in Belfast's Royal Avenue, just half a mile from the front gates of City Hall, on the night of 15 December 1991.

The hacks and others in the *BelTel* used it as a watering hole. I did so myself. A portrait of regulars by County Down artist Quigley, in which I am included, was prominently displayed on the back wall.

But this night, Colm Mahon had spotted a team of drug-dealers in the club. He told them he wanted them out. They threatened him, so he told them they were barred. As they were leaving through the main door, one of them turned to Colm and told him he was going to get a gun, to come back, and shoot him dead.

Ten minutes later, that is exactly what happened.

The INLA terrorist who was ordered to take the rap for that was one Christopher 'Crip' McWilliams. 'Crip' McWilliams was later to lead the three-man gang which carried out the audacious 1997 killing of LVF Godfather Billy 'King Rat' Wright behind bars in Maghaberry jail. Sentenced to twenty years in 1998, McWilliams served only two years before being released under the terms of the Good Friday Agreement.

The word on the street was that it was in fact, another INLA man—who later fled to Australia with a suitcase full of INLA money—who shot dead utterly defenceless Colm Mahon at point blank range.

Now, I was being threatened with the same fate, in this downtown Belfast bar, with the blazing turf fire. And I knew the thug threatening to go for the gun was part of the same INLA gang which had murdered Colm Mahon.

As the drug-dealer strode purposefully towards the door, I went after him. My intention was to have a go at him in the alleyway outside, creating the chance for myself and my friends to do a runner. But I was concerned that the ex-police officer who was due to meet us in the bar would dander (stroll) into this 'gang' on his own, anyway.

I needn't have worried. Just as I got out into the entry on the drug-dealer's heels, the big former cop, his angular frame casting a long shadow in the street lights, came striding down the entry, his trademark Crombie overcoat flapping open, as usual, like angel's wings in the wind. But this big lad was no Angel of Mercy. Indeed, he had been more of an Avenging Angel to quite a few top terrorists, on both sides, during the Troubles. This is why, even though retired from the police force, he still carried a PPW—Personal Protection Weapon. I'm not revealing his identity here: for 'security reasons', you understand, but let's just call him 'Big Mac': he could weigh up and eat up criminals faster than any of them could scoff a similarly named burger out of a McDonald's.

'What's the problem?' 'Big Mac' demanded as I 'pulled' the drugs dealer.

'This arsehole says he's going to get a gun and shoot me,' said I.

At which point, 'Big Mac' pulled out his own weapon, stuck the barrel right up the drug-dealer's right nostril, and told him: 'You don't go back into that bar now, sonny, and set your arse back down with your cronies, I'll blow your brains the whole way back to where you came from. Understood?'

Yer man 'understood'. But it might have been different, a lot different, if he had actually had the gun he was threatening to get at that moment.

'Big Mac' and I followed him into the bar, and then jointly issued that two-word Belfast phrase better known than any other throughout the Troubles. 'Everybody out!' we told our friends inside. And we scarpered out of that bar faster than rats up a dark entry.

———

But, to use another oul' Ulster saying, 'the war wasn't over' as far as that incident was concerned. We may have won the battle then, but, you can guess the rest.

Two days later, I'm sitting in work. It's about 8.15 a.m. I'm breaking another safety rule the police have given me: 'Stop going into that office on your own early in the morning with no one else there.' Well meant as it is, that's an impossible rule to observe most of the time: there's a lot of paperwork in my job: legals, correspondence, the everyday running of the office, and it's better to get that done before the rest of the staff come in and the phones start going bananas, as is the daily norm in a paper as busy as ours.

Anyway, 8.15 a.m., I'm in the office on my own, working on yet another (spurious) complaint filed by lawyers who really should know better, representing some criminal lowlife who we have exposed, and who now wants us reported to the Press Complaints Commission in London. It is 10 November 2003.

I answer the phone to a police inspector based at Lisburn Road barracks in south Belfast. This station covers the area where our office is situated in downtown Belfast. The inspector—who, it turns out, went to the same school as myself—says he needs to come down and see me: 'urgently' is the word he uses.

I suspect another threat. He confirms it, but says, as usual, he cannot discuss it over the phone. He'll be down to see me in half an hour.

He is. In full uniform, but again, he's 'just passing the message on, as required'. By this stage, I know this is all uniformed police officers can do even though they may have gone to the same school as you.

Handwritten in capital letters on the PM1 'Confidential' police form, the message was short, but not at all sweet. It was stark and shocking, and the name on it was my own. The address was that of the *Sunday World*. The message read:

'EDITOR OF *SUNDAY WORLD*, THEY PLAN TO SHOOT HIM THIS MORNING.'

I looked at the big, friendly cop. 'You know what you need to do,' he said.

I did. I printed my name on the bottom of the warning form, and then signed it. The police inspector signed the form in my presence, to prove I'd got it. We shook hands. He left.

I phoned Lindy who was in work up at the *Telegraph*, a couple of minutes' dander from our office off Donegall Street. 'Have you got a minute? I need to see you about something,' I said.

'It's not another threat?' she asked, instinctively knowing that it was.

'I'll see you for a cup of tea. Ten minutes?'

We met across the road from the *'Tele'*. In the front part of Frames pub/club, where people meet in the mornings for tea or coffee breaks and a wee jam bun, the same pub where Colm Mahon had been cut down in cold blood by INLA drugs dealers.

Now, I knew, without being told by the police, that the same team were threatening me. Had to be, after what had happened in the old pub-up-the-entry with the turf fire a couple of nights ago.

Lindy did a double take when I showed her the form. 'What the hell are you doing out?' she said. 'Why didn't you stay in the office? It says here they're going to shoot you this morning. So you come out onto the street to give them a chance! Wouldn't you have been safer staying in the office until noon at least?'

As we had our tea she kept glancing at her watch, counting down until noon—when presumably the 'morning' deadline would be over! She was making light of the threat—it's how we've always treated them. You take any death threat seriously—you'd be a fool not to—but you have to retain a sense of humour to keep your sanity.

'Right, I'm going back to work,' I said when we'd finished our tea. 'See you later.'

'Well, hopefully…' she replied.

I'll tell you, folks, that particular High Noon was a long time coming…

17 | SPOOKED!

I went to college with the renowned author Martin Dillon, now resident in New York. We both studied journalism in the late '60s along with big Ivan Little of UTV, his co-station colleague Gary Gillespie and David McKittrick of the *Independent*, to name just a smattering of our collegiate, or 'colleejits' as we were wont to call ourselves.

But Dillon pegged, once and for all, the undercurrents of what was happening in this country when he penned his bestseller entitled *The Dirty War*. This book delved and dived deep into the mire—'murky waters' is too soft a cliché—of intelligence agents, touts, double agents and double-crossings during the Troubles.

Over the years, a lot of what Dillon documented has come under the microscope, with a virtual carpet-bombing of official inquiries, some of which are still running, both North and South of the border, ordered by both the British and Irish governments. Some internal probes have also been sanctioned by the chiefs of both the police and army serving in Ulster.

Internal investigations—especially into suspected touts, or informers—have also long been the mainstay of all the major paramilitary organisations. The Provos had their so-called 'Nutting Squad', led by Freddie 'Stakeknife' Scappaticci, which hunted down and then summarily executed suspected spies in IRA ranks 'convicted' in kangaroo courts. Both main loyalist terror gangs, the UDA and the UVF, had something similar, though on a more random and localised basis than the Provos' centralised system of just one internal investigation unit, or cell.

So it was more than ironic when the head of the IRA's 'Nutting Squad', Freddie Scappaticci, was himself exposed as a British agent. To use a word much favoured by Gerry Adams, that sparked a 'seismic' upheaval in IRA ranks.

But a 'seismic' event is one thing. A tsunami is quite another. And the tsunami which rolled over the IRA came when, not long after Scappaticci was exposed, another ultra-senior republican, Denis Donaldson, confessed to having been a British agent for over twenty years! Along with the Scappaticci revelation, the Donaldson tsunami amounted to a 'traitors-in-the-ranks' double whammy. And at the highest level in the IRA/Sinn Féin axis, too.

Eventually, Scappaticci was to 'do a runner', and return to the country from which his family of ice-cream sellers had originally come, Italy. He needed to escape the team of killers he had once headed up: the 'Nutting Squad'. Why was he allowed to 'do a runner'? the word on the street is that he knew too many secrets about other IRA men and high-profile Sinn Féiners. And that he left behind a life-insurance policy in Belfast: an affadavit, naming certain people, lodged with a lawyer. Just in case.

Donaldson wasn't so lucky. He was to end up on a marble mortuary slab for his 'betrayal', the terms of which are spelt out, graphically, in the IRA Army Council's little green book of 'Rules'. The *Sunday World* was to get the finger pointed at it for its alleged role in Donaldson's demise, too. But more of that later.

Donaldson, originally from the Short Strand area of east Belfast, was a lifelong republican and IRA man who had held posts in Sinn Féin directing international affairs and relationships with other 'revolutionary' groups around the globe. He'd also been their administration boss when they took seats in the power sharing government at Stormont, set up under the Good Friday Agreement of Easter 1998.

But all of that began to unravel four years later. At the start of autumn 2002 rumours of a republican 'spy ring' operating at the very heart of the power-sharing assembly at Stormont began to circulate among the media. In the first week of October that same year, the police swooped dramatically. Boiler-suited anti-terror cops raided Sinn Féin's offices at the seat of the fledgling devolved government. Two computer disks were seized and removed from Sinn Féin offices.

This raid gave rise to the whole spying drama dubbed 'Stormontgate' in the Press. The operation was conducted under a blaze of publicity. And it sparked uproar—on both sides of Ulster's political divide. On the one hand, the Shinners were screaming: 'Set up!' On the other, Ian Paisley's DUP and the Ulster Unionist Party of the then First Minister, David Trimble, were baying: 'Betrayal!'. The scandal would eventually bring down the power-sharing ruling executive and the assembly when Secretary of State John Reid pulled the plug on the by-then hopelessly deadlocked parties.

Before that, however, Donaldson's modest home in West Belfast was also raided by heavily armed cops decked out in black 'Ninja'-style battle gear. Thousands of documents were seized. He, his son-in-law Ciaran Kearney and a former porter at Stormont, William Mackessy, were all lifted, questioned and charged as part of this 'Stormontgate' spy ring.

The PSNI put in place a huge operation informing thousands of people that their personal details were 'believed to have been

gathered and held by the Provisional Irish Republican Army'.
I know. I was one of them. Warnings went out to police officers, prison wardens, other members of the security forces,
civil servants, officers of the courts, and other individuals.
It apparently took a marathon operation to sift through all
the information gathered in the 'thousands of documents'
seized.

My official 'police message', Ref No. OH/O/037/03, was deliv-
ered to me at work at 11.15 a.m. on 9 August 2003 (coinciden-
tally, the anniversary of internment), almost a year after the
'Stormontgate' raid. It was delivered on behalf of the Regional
Assessment Unit, c/o Assistant Chief Constable Urban Region,
PSNI Station Castlereagh. It read, in black bold print at the top:

> '**MESSAGE**: During a search of premises in Belfast on
> 4 October 2002 Police took possession of a quantity of
> documents. Examination of the documents has revealed
> information relating to you. The following is a copy of the
> extract relating to you.'

4 October… the same day Denis Donaldson's house was raided
in the wake of 'Stormontgate'. Most of the rest of the content of
what apparently was in the Provo document 'relating' to me
concerned a report I had written for the paper on 7 November
2001, five weeks after our colleague Martin O'Hagan's murder
by the LVF in Lurgan. It read:

> '*Sunday World* 07.10.2001. Jim McDowell [sic] claims knows
> identity of trio who killed O'Hagan (claimed by Red Hand
> Defenders), LVF 3 terrorising Lurgan, German gun used also
> killed Graham Marks, Tandragee, Co. Armagh, part of
> LVF/UVF feud.'

There's a line I'm leaving out here about Martin O'Hagan, because it's not true: it wasn't in anything I or anybody else wrote for the *Sunday World* about him or his murder, and it's the first time I had seen, or heard, such an allegation. But it makes me think the Provos were adding their own 'intelligence' to what we were writing at the time. The rest of the text of what was allegedly in the Provo file read that after Martin's murder:

> 'Loyalists celebrated in pub used by Billy Wright. One of the 3 threw punch at O'Hagan in recent Craigavon court case. Same runner, hood based in Dungannon, string of minor convictions, who supplied gun in killing of UVF Portadown Richanrd [sic] Jameson and started feud supplied gun for O'Hagan, got it from 2 LVF brothers based in Antrim town.'

The final line read, 'Links between C Company and Mid-Ulster LVF very close, recent meetings between leaders in Shankill'.

The reference to C Company is obviously Johnny 'Mad Dog' Adair's mob on Belfast's Shankill Road. Now, I didn't write that line in anything on 7 November 2001. I didn't know about it at the time. But the Provos must have been doing their homework. This report of theirs was obviously written well before 4 October 2002, when it was apparently seized in the post-Stormontgate police raids.

And wasn't it in the red-hot summer of 2002 that 'Mad Dog' and his cohorts marched down the Shankill, flaunting an LVF flag in front of the UVF gathered outside the Rex bar—and obviously mocking the murder of Richard Jameson in Portadown by the LVF, which sparked a huge riot and then a running and bloody internecine feud with the UVF which was ultimately to cost eight lives on both sides?

If the authenticity of the document allegedly put together by the Provos was in question, there is one thing for certain: they were certainly well up to the mark there.

As it was, at the end of the warning form of which I took possession and signed at 11.15 a.m. on 9 August 2003, again printed in bold letters, came the words: 'This information is believed to have been gathered and held by the Provisional Irish Republican Army. You are advised to seek advice on and take steps to protect your personal security.'

The two computer disks removed by police from Sinn Féin's Stormont offices were later returned to Sinn Féin. But Denis Donaldson was never to return to Stormont. Just over three years after the 'Stormontgate' affair, on 8 December 2005, it was announced that all charges were being dropped against Donaldson, then 55, his son-in-law Ciaran Kearney, and William Mackesson.

The Unionists railed. They claimed it was a 'pay-off' for the Provos, chaperoned by Catholic priest Fr Alex Reid and Protestant clergyman the Rev Harold Good, revealing the decommissioning of their weapons three months earlier. That announcement was officially read out on 25 September 2005, by the head of the international decommissioning body, retired Canadian General Sir John de Chastelain. It was jointly hailed by the then British Prime Minister Tony Blair and the then Taoiseach Bertie Ahern as a major breakthrough.

Just eight days after the charges against the 'Stormontgate' trio had been dropped came the bombshell. On 16 December 2005 Gerry Adams chose Dublin as the venue to announce that Donaldson was being 'expelled' from his political party, confirming that he had been a British spy for over twenty years. Adams cited MI5 then. In a TV interview later, Donaldson was to claim Special Branch as his employers. Whatever, speculation ran rife about a number of things.

First, had the case really collapsed on 8 December because the authorities already knew Donaldson was a tout? Was Donaldson surfacing as a spy now to cover up for a more senior figure in the Provos/Sinn Féin, who knew all about him and Freddie 'Stakeknife' Scappaticci, now conveniently in self-imposed exile? And who had 'turned' Donaldson, a dyed-in-the-wool republican, all those years ago and why?

Our sources in *Sunday World* pointed to two possible factors. Donaldson had been a known womaniser, right throughout his time in the 'Ra and Sinn Féin. Perhaps he had been compromised in a 'honey-trap' sex-sting operation by MI5, and virtually been blackmailed into turning tout. Another possibility was that perhaps he had a relative who was once in bad trouble with the RUC, and he had traded himself as an undercover agent for this relative's freedom from charges.

Whatever the reason, Donaldson took it to his grave with him. For, just like Scappaticci before him, he, too, 'did a runner' to save his skin. Only he didn't run far enough. Donaldson headed over the border, bunkering down in a wee dundering-in of a cottage in need of repair near Glenties in County Donegal. The ex-Provisional was living like a hermit, only venturing into nearby Glenties for subsistence provisions.

Among the foothills of Donegal, he had gone off the radar: gone to ground, amid a complete media blackout.

That blackout was breached by *Sunday World* reporter Hugh Jordan during the last week of March 2006. Hugh, originally from Glasgow, spent his childhood holidays in the Gaeltacht of Donegal. He loves the place. Has written songs about it. And, more importantly given his profession, has many contacts up there.

He tracked Donaldson down to this isolated cottage. He wanted Donaldson to tell, in his own words, his own story. Donaldson was affable with Hugh, but evasive. Hugh filed his report, job well done, when he came back to Belfast. With the first, exclusive pictures of Donaldson outside his Donegal hide-away cottage accompanying it—we splashed with the story on Page 1 two days after St Patrick's Day, on Sunday 19 March 2006.

The apt, and accurate headline in huge, bold capital letters across the front page, and accompanied by film-clip-style footage of Donaldson—he had been filmed on a camcorder—simply read:

SPOOKED
Sinn Féin super spy Denis Donaldson has swapped the corridors of power for a squalid Donegal hovel.
This week the *Sunday World* tracked the former MI5 agent to his tumble-down Donegal hideaway—a world away from the days when as a trusted aide to Gerry Adams he travelled the globe as a top Sinn Féin official.

Covering the story and pictures over three pages inside, we ran two headlines. The first over a double-page spread pointing out that the bolthole cottage had no electricity or running water read: WE SPY DONALDSON. On the third page we carried a picture of Donaldson on the H Blocks in Long Kesh with the first IRA hunger striker to die in 1981, Bobby Sands.

The headline on that read:

SPYMASTER WAS SANDS' BEST PAL

Hugh's interview with Donaldson was short but remarkable and revelatory in a number of respects, not least about the documents which had been discovered in his house, and which led to the police warning to me.

The first question Donaldson asked Hugh was, 'How did you manage to find this place. You don't see much of anyone here.'

He added: 'I don't be in touch with anyone. As you can see, I'm in the middle of nowhere.'

Asked about his plight, he tried to pin the blame for his 'outing' as a spy on a political plot to keep David Trimble of the UUP in pilot position on the Unionist side, instead of Ian Paisley of the DUP. In the wake of 'Stormontgate', he point-blank denied that there had ever been a Sinn Féin spy ring operating at the seat of the power-sharing Assembly. And as to the discovery of that holdall in his west-Belfast home, which contained sensitive documents relating to the British Army chief-of-staff as well as hundreds of prison officers and other individuals—including details about me—Donaldson said: 'I never saw that bag in my life before.'

However, Donaldson did claim the bag belonged to his son. He told Hugh: 'There was nothing to connect me to it—neither my fingerprints nor my DNA was on it, but I took responsibility for it because my wife and son were in the house. I knew nothing of that bag and I've no idea how it got into my house.'

And one thing he said to Hugh in the brief interview outside his front door was to prove prophetic: he denied that he was on the run, from the IRA or anyone else. 'I'm not hiding. I just want to be left alone. I don't go anywhere,' he morosely stated.

Well, he should have been in hiding. There was little chance of him being left alone, given his past, so he should have 'done a runner' overseas, like Freddie 'Stakeknife' Scappaticci before him. Because around twilight on Tuesday 4 April 2006, just four months after Gerry Adams unmasked him as a British spy, Denis Donaldson was gunned down at the front door of his cottage in the most gruesome way: with a shotgun. The shotgun was used because unlike assault rifles or handguns, it leaves no telltale forensic evidence: the cartridge disintegrates as it blasts the life out of the killer's victim. It is, in spite of the contradictory nature of the term, a 'clean gun', and it has been used by the IRA before, especially in the murders of some drug-dealers.

As for us, as speculation about 'whodunnit' spiralled, we had no doubt. The following Sunday 9 April, we blew a big hole in the speculation, running a front-page banner headline which read:

PROVOS DID KILL MI5 SPY
Hardliners told IRA chiefs Donaldson had to die.

We cited two reasons for that. First, Donaldson had broken the main rule in the IRA 'little green book': no one turns tout. There were suspicions in Provo ranks that having been an MI5 or Special-Branch spy for over twenty years, he could have set up ambushes for the SAS and provided information to the authorities on both sides of the border which led to operations like the huge raid on former IRA Army-Council boss Thomas 'Slab' Murphy's criminal empire HQ in South Armagh. We pointed out that Murphy's mob, in particular, would have had a lust for revenge had this come to light.

The second reason was that the Provos in East Tyrone had long memories about the Loughgall ambush in County Armagh in 1987, which took out eight of their top volunteers, including their then OC, Jim Lynagh.

Hugh Jordan had been the first journalist to find, and interview, Donaldson at his Donegal cottage bolthole. The cold-blooded assassination came just two weeks after. Innuendo and accusation immediately surfaced about the *Sunday World* being in some way responsible for Donaldson's demise. Those were dangerous, and in some cases despicable, claims, some of them coming from people who should have known better. Hugh felt so angry about one in particular that he instigated legal action. After all, the IRA are no mugs: their 'intelligence' would have pin-pointed where Donaldson had bolted to—from the minute and hour he arrived at the Donegal hovel.

Meantime, both Hugh and I had to parry questions from other sections of the media: and some of those questions were as blunt and abrasive as the sliotar hit by Cúchulainn which stuck in the attacking hound's throat.

One in particular, on Stephen Nolan's talk show the morning after Donaldson was discovered dead, was a choker. As Editor of the Northern edition of the *Sunday World*, the Nolan Show asked me on to talk about the killing. By this time, both Hugh and I were just about saturated with the whole affair: the original 19 March 'SPOOKED' story had sparked a media feeding frenzy. And, because of who Denis Donaldson was, there were security issues, again. Nothing formal, but there were a lot of Chinese whispers, and whisperers, about the place.

Now, Stephen was just doing his job as usual: going for the jugular, in other words. But while I regard him as a mate, there was nothing matey about the first question hurled my way on his show that morning. 'Does the *Sunday World* have blood on its hands?' he asked. As subtle as a shipyard worker's welding iron...

I told him, just as I had to tell a platoon of other verbal pugilists that day, that we definitely didn't. I told him that Hugh Jordan had gone to chase a legitimate story in the public interest. I told him that Denis Donaldson had gone to ground after confessing to being a spy and that people wanted to know why: why he had become a spy in the first place, and why he was still living in Ireland when everyone—including himself—knew the ultimate price for being an informer in IRA ranks. The pursuit and publication of the Donaldson story was sanctioned and carried out for the best possible motives: in the public interest. That is what the *Sunday World* is about: telling the public what other people—politicians, paramilitaries, whatever—don't want them to know. Enough said.

In any case, in the context of the 'SPOOKED' story, if we knew where Donaldson was, the Provos, after all their years of gathering intelligence (a lot of it for the precise purpose of murdering their targets) certainly did.

However, that interview—I parted from Stephen in the studio after shaking his hand as usual—signalled the start of another storm which broke over the Donaldson slaying. We weathered it, as usual, and it had largely blown over by the time of Denis Donaldson's funeral back home in west Belfast four days after his assassination.

The funeral took place on Saturday, 9 April 2006. Our double-page spread inside the paper the next day carried the headline:

IRA KILLED DONALDSON

At the end of that report, we carried three paragraphs. They read:

> Meantime, Denis Donaldson made the final leg of his journey home from exile in County Donegal back to where he had lived in West Belfast yesterday.
>
> He was buried in the City Cemetery in the west of the city, after a private Mass at a Catholic church close to the city centre.
>
> Significantly, none of the leading republicans, including Gerry Adams, who had been his comrades when he was head of the Sinn Féin administration at Stormont, or their director of international affairs, attended the funeral.

In the context of our editorial line that the Provos *did* kill Denis Donaldson, that word 'Significantly' at the start of the last paragraph was very significant indeed…

And there was one other salient and 'significant' fact attached to the whole saga. Although we pinned the blame for Donaldson's death on the Provos, and they posted a general denial—well, they would, wouldn't they?—there was no specific denial to us in the *Sunday World*. No one contacted us directly. There were no complaints conveyed to me. And there was no official complaint to the Press Complaints Commission about our coverage of the Donegal cottage slaying. This killing bore the classic hallmarks of a Provo 'No Claim No Blame' murder. It wasn't 'sanctioned' by the Army Council, so, on paper at any rate, it wasn't the IRA. Also, they used a gun which would leave no forensic evidence. And our sources pointed to the killers coming from the IRA strongholds of either Armagh or Derry. In the eyes of these hardliners, Donaldson had committed 'treason'. And the sentence for that, in the IRA's Green Book, was death.

The silence which greeted our reports on Donaldson's execution, was in stark contrast to the response to a story which we broke seven weeks after Denis Donaldson was shot dead on his doorstep.

There had been much speculation, both before and after his 'home alone' murder, that Donaldson had 'taken the rap' as a British spy to cover for someone higher up in the republican movement. The reckoning was that to be a tout for all those years, Donaldson would have needed to have cover from a 'minder' in the highest echelons of Sinn Féin and the Provos. Among the names that came into that particular frame were the two at the top: Gerry Adams himself and Martin McGuinness.

In the fourth week of May 2006, former British agent Martin Ingram turned whistleblower. The former spy who 'outed'

Freddie 'Stakeknife' Scappaticci, made another sensational claim, exclusively to the *Sunday World*.

And this time, when we reported Ingram's allegation, there was a reaction that rumbled the length of Derry's famous walls. There was an official complaint to the Press Complaints Commission, and there was another official warning from the police of a threat. This time from the IRA.

18 | MARTIN McGUINNESS: THE 'SPY' SAGA

The front-page headline on Sunday 28 May hit harder than a Barry McGuigan left hook to the ribcage. In capital letters it clarioned:

McGUINNESS WAS BRIT SPY

Above it, in a panel at the top beside the *Sunday World* masthead, we ran a 'qualifying' sub-head. It read:

SPOOK'S SHOCK CLAIMS

That made clear that it was not the paper which was claiming Martin McGuinness was a spy. It was someone else. What we were doing was reporting the allegation. And in the copy which accompanied the front-page 'write-off' on the story inside, journalist John Cassidy wrote: 'Sinn Féin chief Martin McGuinness is named today as a high-ranking MI6 agent at the heart of the IRA. The explosive revelations are made by a former agent handler in the shadowy Force Research Unit, Martin Ingram. Freddie Scappaticci was also unmasked two years ago by the same agent as the FRU agent 'Stakeknife', who was a senior figure in the IRA.'

The wording of both the headlines—and especially the 'Spook's Shock Claims' sub-head—and the write-off were to prove crucial subsequently. Because Martin McGuinness, after an uncharacteristically lengthy silence on his part, was to rubbish the claim, and our story, in other media outlets. He was also to take us to the Press Complaints Commission. And lose. But more of that later.

As it was, our story carried claims from Martin Ingram that McGuinness had an MI6 handler known to him as 'G', and the senior Shinner's codename was 'J118'. Ingram claimed to have seen the transcript of a conversation between 'G' and 'J118' in which extending the IRA's 'human bomb' campaign against British Army checkpoints and barracks was encouraged. The idea was to provoke a public backlash against the Provos, especially in mainland Britain.

MI6 allegedly wanted this to happen and was encouraging McGuinness to get the Derry Brigade of the Provos to carry out more of those attacks. (McGuinness has since publicly admitted, of course, that he was 2nd Officer Commanding of the IRA's Derry Brigade.)

Previously, in October 1990, Derryman Patsy Gillespie, 42, had been used as a 'human bomb' when he was forced to drive a van packed with explosives to a military-vehicle checkpoint at Coshquin on the border with Donegal. The huge bomb detonated while Mr Gillespie, whose 'crime' in the IRA's eyes was working in army bases to earn a living, was still in the driver's seat. He died along with five soldiers from the King's Regiment manning the checkpoint.

Martin Ingram claimed that the door to the cab was booby-trapped. He said: 'A device was wired to the light inside the cab. Once Patsy opened the door to the truck the device went off.'

This story also carried other claims by Martin Ingram. But the core of it was his allegation that Martin McGuinness was a spy for the 'Brits'. Ingram said that he had for long harboured a suspicion that the Sinn Féin boss in Derry was an intelligence agent. He was now stating categorically: 'This transcript, which is a hundred per cent authentic, proves to me that McGuinness was working for MI6.'

So, a proven 'whistleblower' in the Scappaticci spy revelation had the Provos whistling into the wind: again. They rallied to McGuinness's side and to blow away Ingram, in a figurative sense, in a whirlwind of propaganda aimed at undermining his reputation.

The storm reached its peak the following Friday, but in two very different ways. Speaking at an Irish-language school on 2 June 2006, Gerry Adams claimed that Ingram's aim was to get Martin McGuinness blown away, in a physical sense. He denigrated the claim that McGuinness was an MI6 agent as 'absolute rubbish', stating: 'What I would be concerned about is that there is another agenda involved here and in fact every time there is an effort to move the [political] process forward, or at this stage to move the institutions into being again, there have always been interventions.

'The sub-text of all of this is that there is a possibility that elements within there want to see Martin McGuinness dead.

'That's what I take out of this. It is a very serious situation. I think it is emanating from the old guard within the old RUC, perhaps some still active in the PSNI and all the dirty tricks within British military intelligence.'

The Adams outburst was relayed to Ingram, living in a secret hideaway for his own protection. His reaction was typically belligerent and obstinate. He told our reporter, John Cassidy: 'His [Adams'] remarks are aimed at me and anybody who knows me knows that what he is saying is not true.' He added:

'What I want to see happen to Martin McGuinness is what I have wanted to see happen to Freddie Scappaticci. Why is the British State protecting Martin McGuinness? Why is it not in the public interest to prosecute Martin McGuinness? I'll tell you why: because Martin McGuinness was the *crème-de-la-crème* of agents [that was] working for British intelligence. I stand over what I said last weekend: Martin McGuinness was working for MI6.'

As Adams and Ingram were rolling with the punches in that verbal scrap that Friday, I was on my way into east Belfast. The previous night, I had been contacted, through an intermediary, by a man I knew to have been a very senior intelligence agent throughout the Troubles. He had narrowly escaped a number of attempts on his life and he had been a bane to both the IRA and all factions of loyalist terror gangs for one reason: they feared him. Which is why they had both tried to kill him: frequently.

Anyway, a go-between had told me that this man wanted to meet me. He said the intelligence agent 'had more' on the McGuinness story. And 'more' on other 'intelligence agents/informers/touts, call them what you will' working within and across a phalanx of Ulster's paramilitary organisations. He said this man didn't want money. Martin Ingram hadn't either, and we'd made that clear, in print, as a 'rider' at the foot of the first John Cassidy story.

What this man wanted to do, said the go-between, was to 'set the record' straight on what the senior intelligence officer was later to say 'really was a dirty little war.'

I said I'd meet the source. I was given instructions where to go the next day, Friday, and told not to bring my own car, but to borrow one whose make and registration may not be known by the security sources. I was told to go to a car park in the Belfast area and just wait, and that I would be watched.

I did all of that. I was sitting in the car when my mobile rang. I was told to get out of the car and go to a certain house. Another person I knew—but not the senior security man—answered the door. I was ushered inside.

My contact, the senior intelligence agent referred to by the go-between the night before, was sitting in that room. Other people who the security man knew were in the house. I knew some of them. None of them was in the police or army.

It looked as though I had just dropped in for a cup of tea. We talked about sport over a cup of tea and then I said I had to go. As I walked down the hallway, the contact came after me. 'I'll follow you over to the car,' he said, pointedly adding: 'I see you're not driving your own motor today.'

That was that checked out…

He got into the passenger seat and produced a small notebook. There was a list of names inside, with a list of codenames written beside them. I glanced at the first name. Martin McGuinness. 'That's only the first,' said the contact. 'There are others.'

He began to flick through the pages. I stopped him. I asked him to get out of the car, leave the notebook with me, go back to the house and get whoever had my mobile number to ring me in five minutes. I didn't want this contact's number in my phone or on my person. And I also didn't want both of us sitting in the car with that notebook: someone else in the murky underworld of the secret service might nail both of us red-handed with some ultra-sensitive stuff.

He agreed to go back to the house, but not before going round to the driver's window, getting me to roll it down and then leaning in and plucking the car keys from the ignition. Just in case. But then maybe that's why he had reached the rank that he had: and, more importantly, why he had escaped myriad murder bids.

I was left with the notebook and the dynamite details inside. I took out my own notebook and copied into it the names and codenames from his.

Five minutes later, my mobile rang. 'Are you done?' asked the voice on the other end, not that of the senior intelligence officer. I said yes, and the intelligence agent himself came back over to the car. He got in. I handed him back the wee notebook and thanked him.

As I have already noted, I knew this man, and therefore was sure about his authenticity at the heart of intelligence-gathering for years. Indeed, there was one element of how he operated—'calling in' touts if their handlers thought the informers had been compromised and their lives were in danger—that was intriguing, but would be a dead giveaway if I revealed it here, with the emphasis on the word 'dead'.

But I wanted to know what had spurred him to get in touch with me at this time. My contact said it was not our Martin McGuinness story of the previous Sunday itself, but the reaction to it, which had prompted him to make contact. He said that it was 'time the lid was lifted' on the whole spying story between British intelligence agencies—including the police Special Branch in Ulster—and republican and loyalist paramilitaries.

And just as Martin Ingram did that Friday in the wake of the Gerry Adams claim, the source sitting with me insisted: 'I'm not trying to set anyone up for targeting or death, as some people have suggested this week. But this really was a dirty little war. And if we're talking about the war really being over, it's better that everything should come out in the wash now, rather than later, if there really is going to be a peace process involving truth and reconciliation.'

But I needed to flesh out more details on the skeleton of the notes we now both had in our possession. Still in the car, he obliged. That done, he handed me back the car keys, got out, and walked back to the house.

I drove away. Quickly, but warily. However, I wanted to look at my own copy of what I'd cogged from the source's own wee notebook. I pulled into another car park. Nobody noticed or bothered with me.

Marrying what was in the notebook to what the source told me, this is his story:

First, the codename notated beside that of Martin McGuinness, was 'The Fisherman'. It seemed apt, but obvious. After all, McGuinness was a keen angler. My source claimed that the self-confessed 2nd OC of the Derry Brigade of the IRA worked to a British intelligence unit known as 'Box 500'. This covered, he said, MI5, MI6 and the British Army's undercover Force Research Unit (the aforementioned FRU). And the other angle on McGuinness's codename 'The Fisherman'? FRU's motto happens to be 'Fishers of Men'.

For the first time, the source also revealed the codename used by Denis Donaldson. He said it was 'Mr O'Neill'—a play on the pseudonym 'P. O'Neill', the name that traditionally appeared at the end of statements issued by the IRA and was the mark of their authenticity. The source said: 'Those in the IRA who debriefed Donaldson after he admitted he was an informer will know that that is his codename.'

That was just the start. Here's the rest of this short, but potentially explosive, list:

— Someone very close to Brian Keenan, the Provos' one-time deputy chief of staff, also known as the IRA Adjutant General, who died of cancer in May 2008 and was accorded a full IRA 'military' funeral, was a tout.

— Someone equally close to Belfast IRA veteran and jail-breaker Martin Meehan, who became a Sinn Féin politician, was also an informer. Said the source: 'The IRA's North Belfast Brigade met regularly in a flat in the Cliftonville Road area of the city. The flat was wired—bugged—from ceiling to floor. That stopped parts of Belfast being flattened by bombs. The boy [tout] who was involved there was paid half-decent money. We called what he was doing 'preventive medicine'. (Martin Meehan was to die suddenly on Saturday 3 November 2007 from a fatal heart attack, aged 52. At his funeral, his coffin was flanked by IRA men in black berets and black ties—in spite of Sinn Féin sitting in Stormont alongside Paisley's DUP and 'peace' allegedly reigning—Gerry Adams said of him: 'When it was time to wage war, he waged war. When it was time to build peace, he built peace.')

The day before Meehan's funeral, the *Daily Mirror* had run a story saying that Meehan was the executioner of three young off-duty Scottish soldiers lured to their deaths in Belfast in the early 70s. Two of them were eighteen years of age, the other twenty-one.

A Belfast docker, Arthur Rafferty, dying of cancer in 2007, had also claimed in the *Sunday World*, just before Meehan's death, that Meehan had lured his father to be shot and fatally wounded in the street by Freddie 'Stakeknife' Scappaticci. Meehan had denied the claim, saying he was in jail at the time. He later issued legal proceedings against the paper, but died within days of us receiving the documents.

Said my security source: 'Martin Meehan took a lot of secrets to the grave with him. No one will ever know how many, or what those secrets were.'

More details followed:

— The IRA OC in the republican hotbed of Andersonstown, west Belfast, at one time was also an informer. His code-name was 'Chiefy', according to the list.

— The IRA OC in Belfast's close-knit New Lodge area was also a tout. Said the source: 'He liked a drink. He was codenamed "AA"—after Alcoholics Anonymous.'

And, to prove it wasn't always one-sided against the Provos, there was a name in the little notebook without a codeword beside it, but which would rock at least one loyalist terror gang to the core—and corps. The name was that of John McMichael, who has become almost an icon in Protestant paramilitary ranks. McMichael was murdered by the Provos just before Christmas 1987, after being set up by UDA gangster Jimmy Craig (McMichael was probing his criminal activities). Craig was later shot dead in the Bunch of Grapes bar in East Belfast—by the UDA—in revenge.

So the code-worded file in the source's wee notebook wasn't big on quantity. But it was twenty-four carat in quality. But where was the corroboration? Well, that's a big word with sometimes less-than-nine-carat substantiation in Ulster's 'Dirty War'. When the Provos' internal investigation unit, known as the 'Nutting Squad'—and headed up by Scappaticci and Donaldson, to name but a couple—were blowing the brains out of alleged informers 'convicted' in kangaroo courts, they didn't care too much about corroboration. Neither did any of the republican or loyalist bogeymen gangs when they were shooting or bombing innocent civilians or each other for that matter. But I checked out a few sources myself: in the security forces and in the ranks of republicanism. No detail in the little notebook was challenged by my research, and no contact has since denigrated my source.

We ran the story: in a 'splash', the front-page lead, and inside. We also ran a comment from Martin Ingram, the first to dub Martin McGuinness a spy in the previous Sunday's paper. We quoted him then as saying: 'I challenge Martin McGuinness today to a live television debate, with no strings attached, to discuss his role as a British agent. If he has nothing to hide, he should face me and let us discuss his involvement with MI6.'

That 'challenge' was never taken up, and still stands to this day.

Shortly after the publication of this piece, I appeared on TV with McGuinness on a politics programme. I had been asked to do a review of the papers. He was in for an interview on the peace process. I was on first, and at the end of my slot, the interviewer turned to me and asked me about the warning myself and John Cassidy had received from the police about an alleged IRA threat to both of us.

Martin McGuinness didn't dance around the subject. He stated, categorically, that there was no threat to myself or to anyone in the *Sunday World* from the IRA. But he seemed to be irked that the message, delivered to the police, had been made public by the *Sunday World*. I had to remind the interviewer that members of Sinn Féin and the IRA weren't slow in running to the Press when the police delivered the same messages to them about alleged loyalist plots to kill them.

I think I made my point.

On a lighter note, Mr McGuinness rode on the back of a *Sunday World* exclusive picture story featuring the then DUP Press Officer and Belfast Councillor Sammy Wilson. I'll not go into all the details, but way back on 19 May 1996, we'd published pages of pictures of the DUP propaganda boss dubbed 'Red Sammy' (because of his working-class background and, to be fair, grass-roots socialist leanings) cavorting around in the nude on holiday.

The page-1 headline clarioned: 'SAMMY BARES IT ALL', beside a picture of Sammy—from behind, but side-faced so it was clear that it was him—wearing nothing but a pair of Moses sandals. Underneath on the front page was a sub-heading: 'Paisley sidekick starkers in the sun'.

There were quite a few pages inside with more pictures and poking fun—rather than being malicious—at Sammy. But it obviously gave Sammy—and his political czar and Moderator of the Free Presbyterian church Ian Paisley—red faces. Sammy saw red. He sent the police to my house that lunchtime. That eventually came to nothing, but he later took us to the High Court for breach of confidentiality and privilege, settled on the court steps—and hasn't looked back since! He's now a Westminster MP on a big salary and expenses, he's a Stormont assemblyman on similar, and he was, until he resigned in 2007, still a member of Belfast Council and two-time Lord Mayor of his native city. The ex-DUP Public Relations guru should have paid us: we made him with all that free PR in '96!

Still, it was a story that ran and ran, as they say. The former Sinn Féin Councillor Máirtín Ó Muilleoir once asked me to speak to kids in an Irish-language class at Culturlann on the Falls Road in Belfast. I talked to them for about an hour. It came to the last question and about six hands shot up. The teacher in charge winked at me as if he knew what was coming. He told the six that he knew all of them wanted to ask the same question. He told one to ask it on behalf of all. And a wee lad says to me: 'Mister, know what all our das and mas really want to know and asked us to ask you?'

Says I, 'No, son, fire away.'

And says the wee lad, 'They want to know where you got them pictures of Sammy Wilson.'

I cracked up laughing. So did the teacher.

'Ah, son,' says I, using an oul' verbal sidestep: 'Just tell them what I told the Peelers when Sammy sent them to my front door. They came through the *Sunday World*'s door in an unmarked brown envelope…'

Two years later at Stormont, at the first meeting of the Assembly after the signing of the Good Friday Agreement, Sammy Wilson and Martin McGuinness were having a go at each other across the floor of the debating chamber (this was when the DUP opposed Sinn Féin even being in the Big House on the Hill, never mind sitting down in government with them as was to happen nine long years later, in May 2007). The debate was being televised. Wilson was sniping at McGuinness, when the latter coolly fired back with a sharp-shooting quip along the lines of, 'Ach, Sammy, it's good to see you with your clothes on for a change!'

I was sitting on the settee at home watching the television debate. I almost fell off it laughing. The long grass in the fields may have tickled Sammy's fancy way back in '96. The Martin McGuinness one-liner certainly didn't two years later in Stormont. But it did mine, and a lot of other people's…

———

Martin McGuinness took us to the Press Complaints Commission—the *British* PCC, please note—following the 'Spy' claim story.

For the record—and it's important that it should be put on the record, given Mr McGuinness's reaction to the story and his later taking up of the post of Deputy First Minister at Stormont—here is the official PCC ruling:

COMPLAINT:
Mr Martin McGuinness complained, through P.J. McCrory & Co. solicitors, to the Press Complaints Commission that

an article published in the *Sunday World* on 28 May 2006 headlined 'McGuinness was Brit Spy' was inaccurate in breach of Clause 1 (Accuracy) and 2 (Opportunity to reply) of the Code of Practice.

The article contained the claims of Martin Ingram, a former agent handler in the Force Research Unit. He said that a transcript of a conversation between 'J118' and 'G', published in the newspaper, was between the complainant and his MI6 handler.

The complainant was concerned that the headline had stated as fact he was a spy, and that the newspaper did not contact him in advance of the publication for an opportunity to comment. The headline, the complainant said, was not justified by the contents of the article, in which Mr Ingram was quoted as speculating that the complainant was a spy. The transcript document was clearly not authenticated by anyone in a position of knowledge.

The newspaper (in reply) said that the full headline was actually 'Spook's Shock Claims: McGuinness was a Brit Spy'. It was therefore clear that the article concerned an individual's opinion on the subject. The article was based on a document which Martin Ingram claimed was a transcript of a conversation between the complainant and his handler, and which had been authenticated by other intelligence sources. Mr Ingram—who the newspaper said was a credible source and the man who had previously identified the FRU agent 'Stakeknife'—also gave a detailed account of the complainant's alleged co-operation with the security forces. The newspaper did not contact the complainant in advance of the publication, as it was aware that he had not previously been willing to offer a comment to it on any issues of controversy. It published a follow-up article containing Gerry Adams' dismissal of the claims in the following week's edition, and offered to publish an interview with the complainant or a statement of his vehement denial.

The complainant considered that the headline 'Spook's Shock Claims' appeared to be separate, and was in a different box, to the main headline. This gave a misleading impression.

DECISION:
Not Upheld.

ADJUDICATION:
It was clearly not within the scope of the Press Complaints Commission—which does not have legal powers of investigation or subpoena—to establish the veracity of the claims contained in the article. Nor was it necessary for the Commission to do so, in order to come to a decision on this complaint under the terms of the Code. The central question was whether the newspaper had clearly distinguished the claims of Martin Ingram as comment rather than fact. The Commission considered that it had. Above the main headline of the front page was a reference to the 'shock claims' contained within the article. Although this was in a separate box to the headline, the Commission considered that it was clear that it referred to the main article.

Furthermore, the Commission noted that the second paragraph of the front page made it clear that 'the revelations are made by… Martin Ingram', and the opening paragraph of the page-four article began: 'A British Army whistleblower today names Sinn Féin chief Martin McGuinness as a high-ranking mi6 agent'. The banner headline for this story was 'allegations about Republican chief's past'.

Taking all this into account, the Commission considered it likely that readers would have recognised that the reference to the complainant as a spy was not a statement of fact but a claim from an intelligence source.

The second issue related to the newspaper's failure to contact the complainant for comment prior to publication. The Commission considered that, in view of the nature of the allegations, the newspaper should have done so, and included the complainant's denial in the first article published on the subject. Nevertheless, the newspaper had taken care to ensure that readers would be aware that the article was based upon information from an alleged official document and a former member of a security organisation, but that the claims had not been otherwise corroborated. The Commission also noted that the newspaper had published the complainant's dismissal of the allegations as 'total and absolute rubbish' the following week. In these circumstances, the Commission considered that the failure to contact the complainant in itself did not mean that the newspaper had failed to take care over the accuracy of the reporting of the allegation.

That said, the complainant himself clearly considered there to be ambiguity in the presentation of the article. The newspaper had responded to this by agreeing to publish either a follow-up interview or a statement making it clear that the complainant vehemently denied the claims that he was an agent. This was within the spirit of conciliation that the Commission encourages. It hoped that the complainant would take up the offer, but taking the coverage as a whole—and given that it was not in a position to determine whether the claims themselves were true—it (the PCC) did not consider that there were any outstanding issues under the Code for it to pursue.

The PPC Adjudication was issued on 3 November 2006. Mr McGuinness didn't appeal it then. He hasn't done so since.

19 | **THEY HAVEN'T GONE AWAY**

Martin McGuinness stated unequivocally in that TV interview that we were under no threat from the IRA. But they hadn't gone away, you know.

The IRA had splintered after Sinn Féin signed up to the Good Friday Agreement in 1998 and two factions had emerged, the Real and the Continuity IRA. And there was still the INLA lurking in the background, seeking to feed off and recruit 'rebel' Provos.

And the threats to us at the *Sunday World*, being picked up by the police and notified to us and being sifted by our sources, came from others in the still-armed-and-dangerous republican movement. Plus, there were some Provos carrying out activities —whether 'sanctioned' or not by the leadership—who didn't fancy our reporting on their continuing criminal activities.

Such was the case sparked off by a savage incident in one of Belfast's most historic pubs, Kelly's Cellars, just five hundred metres from the front gates of City Hall, on 20 February 2005. It was a dark, but dry, Friday night, just around teatime. One of the hardest men in Belfast, Bobby Tohill, a one-time IRA commander on the lower Falls Road, who boasted that he had been a terrorist since the age of twelve, had fallen out with his former Provo comrades—big time. More than that, the forty-seven-year-old had joined the ranks of dissident voices who were opposed to Sinn Féin's 'politicisation' of the IRA.

Tohill was also 'putting himself about a bit' on the streets of west Belfast and elsewhere, and the 'Ra were being pushed, within their own community, to 'do something about' Tohill. Tohill, built like the gates of the Maze jail in which he was once incarcerated, would be hard to put down. It would take more than one man, in other words. But the Provos were used to hunting in packs. (That's how they operated: as was to unfold later with the mob murder of Short Strand father-of-two Robert McCartney at Magennis's, another pub in downtown Belfast, also only metres from the front of Belfast City Hall.)

That Friday night in February 2005, when the Provos decided to move on Tohill, I was working late in the office. A call came in: someone looking for me. 'Get round to the junction of Townsend Street and Castle Street quick,' the caller urged. 'The cops have just rammed a van and there are boys lying face down in the street with the peelers pointing guns at their heads.'

The scene of the action wasn't too far from our office. I was there within three or four minutes. The rammed van was still sitting askew in the street, there were armed cops all over the place—some of them already in white 'forensic' scene-of-crime suits—and two boys were being loaded into a PSNI 'meat wagon' (Land Rover).

Moments earlier, four men—all of them Provos—had been in that van, along with the man they were attempting to kidnap: Bobby Tohill. The kidnap gang had stormed into Kelly's Cellars where Tohill was drinking. They ambushed him, gave him a savage beating, and were taking him to the border to interrogate and then kill him.

We know all this, because we published the full amazing story less than forty-eight hours later, on the following Sunday morning. And who told us all about it? Bobby Tohill himself, lying heavily bandaged in his hospital bed on the Saturday morning with almost a hundred stitches in his head, and bumps and bruises all over the rest of his body.

Our reporter, Paula Mackin, had got a tickle of what hospital Bobby Tohill was in. She headed there.

At the hospital, Paula did a good job of finding out which ward Tohill was in. She simply walked in and, blood still caked on his wounds, he talked. And he told her in no uncertain terms who had tried to kidnap and kill him.

This is what he told Paula, and what we printed, with his hospital bed picture, on the front page of the Sunday paper:

'It was the Provos. If the police hadn't rammed the van I would be dead now.

'The IRA told me they were taking me to the border to torture and execute me.

'It was a bar-room brawl. I was just standing having a drink when they walked in all ballied up [wearing black woollen balaclavas].

'I couldn't see their faces, but I knew they were for me and I knew it was the IRA.

'They told me I was going to be killed. That's why I fought for so long. I have never experienced fear like it in my life,' said this hardened republican who was proud of being a terrorist before he was even a teenager.

Tohill told Paula, standing at his bedside: 'There was four, maybe five of them. They must have known I wouldn't have went easily. They just laid into me with these metal rods, them ones you press a button and a steel rod shoots out.

'They just started beating me around the head. Every time they hit me I thought I had been shot because of the noise. It was so loud, I can still hear it now. It sounded like a gun-shot.

'But I fought back. I knew I had to keep fighting them. If I gave up, I was dead. I don't know how I kept going for so long, but I knew I had no choice.

'In the end they sprayed (pepper) gas in my face. I couldn't see anything. And then everything went blank.

'I knew it was coming, but nothing could have prepared me for it. I didn't know what hit me.

'I can't remember much, but I do remember people shouting that I had been killed. I actually thought at one stage that they were going to beat me to death in the bar.

'They never stopped hitting me. I don't think they cared if they killed me there and then. They just kept hitting me around the head, full force whacks every time. It felt as if my head was about to explode.'

That interview took place in the Royal Victoria Hospital. Within an hour of getting back on to the street, Tohill wasn't talking any more: to the Press, or to the police. A republican source told us at the time: 'Tohill knew it was the only way to keep alive. He basically was told to keep quiet and the IRA would leave him alone.'

But the Provos didn't like us putting it up to them in the way we did: first on the front page and on the same day Tohill had told Paula in hospital, 'It was the Provos', and then to the Chief Constable of the PSNI. Sir Hugh Orde, was due to hold a Press conference on the Saturday morning at an event being held at the Holiday Inn in Belfast's University Street, which I attended. I asked him, point blank, if he thought the Provos were respon-sible. He said that they were.

After the Tohill incident, we didn't get any notification from the police that there was an 'official' threat. But we had plenty of contacts of our own. And the word from them was no-nonsense: 'You need to watch yourselves…'

But our reporting of the Tohill incident, his hospital bedside interview, and what we had found out about the attempt to kidnap and kill him had another twist. The whole saga had sparked political furore, on both sides of the border, and in Britain. The Good Friday Agreement was being reviewed by all of the Northern Ireland parties who'd signed up to it. That stalled when the then Ulster Unionist Party leader David Trimble walked out over the Tohill affair. Sinn Féin, cornered by their continuing connection to the IRA, said the whole peace process was 'in crisis'.

In September 2003, the British and Irish Governments had set up the International Monitoring Commission (IMC) to 'police' the peace process: in other words, to assess the criminality still extant in the ranks of the paraMafia, and to judge if any of the terror gangs were still at their work. The Commission comprised four just men: Richard Kerr, 32, ex-Deputy Director of America's CIA; Former Scotland Yard anti-terror chief John Grieve; local man Lord John Alderdice, a veteran Ulster politician and the recently retired Speaker of the Stormont Assembly, and Joe Brosnan, former civil-service boss of the Dublin government's Department of Justice.

In the wake of the Tohill affair, the two sovereign governments ordered the IMC to meet in what amounted to emergency session. They told the commissioners to investigate and find out if the IRA were involved in the Tohill battering and kidnap. The Commission convened to do just that in the second week of March 2004.

Both Sinn Féin and the IRA said they were boycotting the IMC probe. We weren't. I and two of our reporters had been approached to meet the IMC to tell them what we knew. The meeting was confidential. But let's just say we did as requested. The meeting was scheduled to last half an hour. We were still in the close and confidential—if eyebrow-raising—conclave an hour and-a-half after walking through the doors of their Adelaide Street HQ in downtown Belfast. What we told them was reflected in their next report. We had opened their eyes to what the paramilitary gangs were still up to. They took it on board...

As it turned out, Bobby Tohill, always a man of action rather words, took a bit of umbrage at the *Sunday World* later. He also took his anger out on us, literally. After drinking in a pub near our office all day, he was walking past our front door and he decided to take out a certain piece of his anatomy and pee up against our shutters. But Bobby himself was well pissed at the time. He failed to notice our outside security camera, recording his act, the video footage of which we retrieved the next day and printed a picture of him doing it in the paper!

He wasn't amused. We were. But we've talked to him since and there are no hard feelings.

The same can't be said of some other republicans who we rubbed up the wrong way. Two, in particular, stand out. One is Frankie 'Studs' Lanigan, now based in Drogheda in County Louth. He was renowned in Belfast as a ruthless 'hitman' from the days of savage internal INLA feuding and the bloody vendettas they waged with their erstwhile 'rivals', the Irish Peoples' Liberation Army. Lanigan had survived a 1995 INLA murder bid himself. Like a posse of his ex-paramilitary cohorts, Lanigan turned to drug dealing. And he was to set up one of Ulster's biggest independent drugs Godfathers, Brendan Campbell, for the Provos—to save his own skin.

The Provos had set up an organisation called DAAD (Direct Action Against Drugs) at the time. That killer gang was responsible for the murder of up to a dozen drug-dealers—the likes of Micky 'Moneybags' Mooney, Brendan 'Speedy' Fegan and 'Big Edd McCoy' among them. However, DAAD now wanted Brendan Campbell dead. They told 'Studs' Lanigan that they'd spare his life if he set up his buddy Brendan for assassination.

Lanigan lured Campbell to a pub called The Three Kegs on Belfast's Boucher Road one night when the bar was almost deserted. DAAD gunmen stormed in. Lanigan slipped into a (conveniently empty) stand-up fridge-freezer to get out of the firing line: sources later said this was a pre-arranged part of the murder plot.

But Campbell, a cocky boy, had balls. He escaped up the stairs—tossing ashtrays and bottles, anything he could get his hands on, at the pursuing Provos. He was wounded, but he escaped. He fled the country briefly after hospital treatment, but when he came back, Lanigan himself turned assassin. He waited for Campbell to get out of a car with his girlfriend on Belfast's bohemian Lisburn Road. It was a mild March night in 1998 and Campbell was going to a popular meeting place, Planks bistro, just opposite one of the biggest police stations in Belfast.

He didn't make it. He was gunned down in the street, fatally this time. 'Studs' did the job himself this time: he was the lone assassin. And he is still on a police WANTED list as chief suspect for that and two other murders. One was the point-blank gunning down of bouncer John Knocker on the door of a nightclub at the Glengannon Hotel, just outside Dungannon, County Tyrone, in the early hours of 31 May, also in 1998. The twenty-two-year-old doorman, known as a hard man who had done time in his native Belfast, already knew Lanigan's 'form' when he entered the club. Lanigan had been in the week before, and had been shown the door.

This time, there was a digging match. Lanigan was on the receiving end of a roistering. Battered and bruised, he went out into the car park. An accomplice, Gregory Martin Fox, was sitting in a car. Using Hollywood movie gangster-speak, Lanigan asked him: 'Where's the shooter?' Fox, then twenty-seven, and sentenced later for his part in the murder, handed Lanigan a 9mm pistol. 'Studs' went back to the nightclub and shot John Knocker dead at point-blank range, before fleeing the murder scene. Now living in Drogheda, Lanigan has crossed the border since. We believe that he became a contract killer.

On 3 June 2004, Kevin McAlorum Jnr had just left his kids off at the gates of Oakwood Integrated Primary School at Derriaghy, just south of the City of Lisburn in Co. Antrim. The thirty-one-year-old was the son of Kevin McAlorum, who was once close to the notorious Mickey Mooney drugs clan, mentioned earlier in connection with Geordie Legge.

Like his da, Kevin Jnr was into drugs: both using and selling them. He had also done time and been involved in internecine republican feuding. In 1996, his kid sister, Barbara, had been shot dead in the living room of her own home by the INLA. Later, Kevin Jnr was jailed for sixteen years for possession of a gun used in the murder of an INLA man. He served just three years, getting out of jail under the early-release clause in the Good Friday Agreement of l998.

But just six years later, at the primary school gates, in front of schoolchildren, two executioners coolly walked up to Kevin McAlorum Jnr and shot him stone dead.

We posted Lanigan as one of the chief suspects in that ruthless killing, as well as a reminder that we believed he'd been involved in the slayings of Brendan Campbell and John Knocker. And we reminded our readers that while Lanigan had first set up, and then assassinated Brendan Campbell to save his own skin with DAAD, and while he had shot dead John Knocker in a fit of red rage, the McAlorum murder bore all the hallmarks of a 'contract' killing.

And we got to know about it—again, not 'formally', but through our own contacts.

He didn't like that.

There was another INLA 'veteran' whom, for legal reasons, both here and in the paper, we can only refer to by his *nom-de-plume*, 'Dark Cloud'. He, too, is a ruthless killer. He once gunned down an off-duty policeman in a city-centre bar frequented by gays. He has never been convicted of that. But he was another INLA heavy hitter—in every sense—who turned to the lucrative drugs trade when it suited him, just like his one-time allegedly 'socialist' comrades in Dublin.

We first pinned the murder of the policeman in the old Parliament Bar on him. And then, when many decent local people contacted us, worried about their kids getting access to the drugs 'Dark Cloud' and his cronies were peddling in areas like the city's Ardoyne and New Lodge Road districts, we started exposing those criminal activities.

But the shadow of drugs and other crimes cast by 'Dark Cloud' still hangs over those areas. In times past, the Provos would have taken him and his gang on: just like their front organisation DAAD did with other drug-dealers. But these days, the Provos are supposedly on ceasefire: that is, if you take the murders of Denis Donaldson and, in 2007, the merciless pummelling to death of Paul Quinn from Cullyhanna on the border out of the equation.

To take on the likes of 'Dark Cloud' and the INLA, the IRA would have to go back to war—temporarily at least. Having allegedly decommissioned all their weapons, what would they have to fight with anyway? And what price, politically, would

Sinn Féin have to pay if they rained all over 'Dark Cloud's' drugs and criminal empire?

Meantime, the letters continue to pour into our office from concerned parents, who are powerless to do anything about him. So they turn to us. As The People's Paper, we try to help those people—and their kids—by continuing to write about 'Dark Cloud' and his criminal fiefdom. In return, we get more visits from the police, and more official warnings that our lives are in danger

I received one such threat, dated 23 July 2003, delivered to my home at 9.25 p.m. Remember, this is over *five years* since the signing of the Good Friday Agreement which was supposed to bring peace to everyone in Ireland, never mind Ulster...

Handwritten in capital letters and signed by a Sergeant at Castlereagh, it read:

INTELLIGENCE INDICATES THAT THERE REMAINS A PHYSICAL THREAT TO *SUNDAY WORLD* EDITOR JIM McDOWELL FROM REPUBLICAN PARAMILITARIES.

And then came the 'bullet point', literally. The writing on the police 'Action Sheet Ref. No. 0703/1793 added:

NEGATIVE ARTICLES ABOUT REPUBLICAN PARA-MILITARY GROUPS WHICH RESULT IN PHYSICAL ATTACKS AGAINST MEMBERS OF THOSE GROUPS MAY RESULT IN POTENTIALLY FATAL ATTACK AGAINST McDOWELL.

Once again, the uniformed sergeant delivering the warning was only doing his job. He couldn't tell me the source of the threat. To be fair, he probably didn't know. Again, it was a case of who-ever picked up that information 'not compromising their source' by being more specific than 'republican paramilitary groups'.

But I knew where it was coming from. And this particular 'Cloud' certainly didn't have a silver lining...

20 | THREATENED – FROM THE GRAVE AND FACE-TO-FACE

Sometimes you don't need anybody to tell you you're under threat. The knowledge and the instinct just descends on you, well, like a dark cloud.

Such was the time we published, on the front page of the *Sunday World*, the first picture to be printed in a newspaper of a terrorist who had haunted us for many years. And who had eventually 'sanctioned' the murder of our reporter, Martin O'Hagan, from the grave.

I've already dealt with the circumstances of Martin's murder in my previous book, *Godfathers*. I've mentioned it in this book, too, in the context of one of the worst terrorists ever to stalk this land, namely Billy 'King Rat' Wright. I have told the story before of how Wright once told his terror gang that if anything happened to him, it was to happen to Martin O'Hagan, 'ten fold'.

Thus it was that Wright's drug-dealing henchmen murdered Martin on 28 September 2001—four years after Wright was gunned down in the Maze Prison two days after Christmas on 27 December 1997.

Those were really rough and tough times for us. And more followed two years later in September 2003. It was then that a potentially deadly dossier came into our hands. It contained details of the official investigation into Wright's murder behind bars. On September 21, we published what we dubbed the 'Dossier of Death' over eleven pages. And on the front, we put the first picture of Wright's gruesome murder scene to be published. Our page-one picture showed Wright lying dead in the back of the white prison van waiting to transfer him from his H-Block to the visiting area of the jail. It was in that van that 'Crip' McWilliams and his murder squad ambushed Wright inside the high-security jail.

Not only the LVF baulked at that. Billy Wright's ex-wife contacted lawyers on behalf of the couple's children. The lawyers reported us to the Press Complaints Commission, claiming we were not interested in acting in the public interest—as we claimed—but were instead 'gloating' over Wright's death. The Press Complaints Commission rejected the complaint. As did the public. We did not have one single complaint from our readers, and didn't drop a single sale the next weekend.

At the end of the day, we were justified in doing what we did way back then in the Autumn of '03. Because as I write this in early 2008, Wright's father, David, has won his long campaign to have a public inquiry staged into the circumstances of his son's murder. A lot of the details we published—and many more—are now being aired in public, and carried by almost every newspaper in the land. And nobody is reporting Mr Wright Snr—or the reporters covering the public inquiry—to the Press Complaints Commission.

However, if ever we needed 'justification' for publishing the details of Wright's demise in the way we did, here's an example. It is the kind of black propaganda the LVF—or, as they came to be known, the 'DVF', for Drugs Volunteer Force—consistently put out about us, trying to blacken the name of the *Sunday World*, and all the journalists and photographers who exposed them for what they were—and are still doing so.

The main hotbed of the LVF founded by Billy 'King Rat' Wright was in the town of Lurgan in Co. Armagh: it still is. And, ironically, much as his mob originally railed at the nickname 'King Rat' bestowed on Wright, they were later to eulogise him with the same pseudonym on almost every wall mural they painted in his memory.

A pamphlet appeared in Lurgan shortly after we published the pictures in 2003, and printed details of the dossier of his death. In big, black bold type it was headed:

SITUATIONS VACANT

Underneath, it advertised for a 'GUTTER-SNIPE JOURNALIST' The poison pen text then read:

'The *Sunday World* is Ireland's premier tabloid; it prides itself in its total lack of integrity, honesty and fairness. A situation has unexpectedly arisen in our Belfast office for a high caliber [sic] gutter-snipe journalist. Due to the cutting edge nature of this post the candidate must demonstrate an exceptional ability to fabricate fantasy-based smear stories against Protestant politicians and paramilitaries. Previous experience in helping to set-up [sic] innocent persons for political assassination would be an advantage, but not essential (on-the-job training will be provided). This is a rare opportunity for an anti-Protestant bigot who can get his/her hands on an NUJ membership card, to play an influential role in undermining the confidence of the Ulster Protestant people and hastening their assimilation into a free 32-county Ireland.'

The pamphlet, A4-sized, stuffed through letterboxes and into shops and circulated widely, then listed 'QUALIFICATIONS', under which read:

'English Language 'O' level grade E or below.

'A prison record—preferably for a scheduled terrorist offense [sic]'.

'Current or former membership of a Republican terrorist murder gang (although special consideration will be given to Pro-Agreement UVF members—if Dictionary Ervine can vouch for them).'

'SKILLS' was the next category listed. Those were catalogued as:

'An aptitude for Black Propaganda coupled with the ability to lie convincingly and take 'credit' for other people's work is a must. Candidates should be aware that in most instances they merely need to pen their name against articles written for them by the NIO, Eire Foreign Affairs Dept, Intelligence Services/RUC Dirty Tricks Department and Pro-Agreement elements of the PUP and any article that Jim McDowell hasn't the balls to put his name to.'

All sinister enough. But then two caveats were added, which were even more so. The first dripped in the kind of 'Black Propaganda' to which the perverted pamphlet itself referred. It read: 'The *Sunday World* is an Equal Opportunity Employer. We will employ anyone who hates Brits and Prods with a passion and who will use their journalistic "skills" to set them up for assassination'.

The second, separate caveat read: 'For further information about this exciting and dangerous mission, apply in your own handwriting (using black or blue crayon only please) to: 'Big

Jim' McDowell (or his successor), *Sunday World*, 3 Commercial Court, Belfast 1. The post is pensionable (if you live that long…)'

All wonderful stuff. Straight out of the handbook of the Nazi propaganda chief Joseph Goebbels who, incidentally, would have fitted comfortably into LVF 'ranks', in both the political and paramilitary senses. But the pamphlet itself fitted into the outlawed categories of both incitement to hatred, and incitement to murder a journalist. The references to myself, or my 'successor', and the post being pensionable 'if you live that long' certainly qualify in the 'incitement to murder' category.

Of course, no one could be prosecuted for either crime. For in spite of the LVF spitting out this litany of lies and inserting the line about me 'not having the balls' to put my name to stories—which I *always* did, and still do—no one in that reptile's nest of neo-Nazi criminals had the balls to put their name to the venomous pamphlet.

And, as late as 2007, the LVF's spawning of yet another generation of kids poisoned by sectarian hatred surfaced yet again. But it was not in pamphlet form this time, printed in black and white on paper and slipped through letter boxes in the dead of night. This time, it was posted on an internet site—by a fifteen-year-old schoolboy! This young man posted a picture of Martin O'Hagan on the internet. He placed a photograph of me on the same site. And he advocated that the same should happen to me as had happened to Martin. 'Out of the mouths of babes' doesn't come into it here.

Still, we gave him a short, sharp shock. We put his picture in the paper. Plus, we made sure the photo of Martin was removed from the particular internet site—and quick, threatening legal action if the internet website didn't spike it immediately.

And we let the police know what was happening. We didn't press for prosecution, though, for a number of reasons, one of which was that there was a danger that if this teenager was arrested, charged and convicted the LVF would make a 'martyr' of him and use that to entice even more teenagers into their organisation and, just as inevitably, into using drugs, being sucked and suckered into working in their vile drugs trade.

But as for other references in that original LVF pamphlet: well, some of them just underpinned their split from, and attitude towards, the Ulster Volunteer Force. Wright, after all, had been kicked out of the UVF under sentence of death. That's why he set up the LVF. And both he and his terror gang always (erroneously and maliciously) punted the line that the *Sunday World* was pro-UVF and pro-PUP—the Progressive Unionist Party, the political wing of the UVF.

Thus their twisted reference under the 'QUALIFICATIONS' segment of the 'SITUATIONS VACANT' pamphlet to 'Pro-Agreement UVF members' and their sideswipe at the man they dubbed 'Dictionary Ervine'. He was, of course, the late David Ervine. And they invented the jibe 'Dictionary Ervine' because not only couldn't they match David Ervine's vocabulary and grasp of the evolving politics of Ireland, North and South, they could hardly string together a few cogent sentences between them, as their pathetic poison-pen pamphlet amply demonstrates.

But then, the LVF weren't the only entity to try to put lives in danger by linking, however loosely, journalists to terror gangs. Indeed, I was to discover that other journalists, perhaps jealous of what we were achieving, tried to paint me with the same brush, and in a very public and pernicious way. Indeed, a certain magazine tried to label me a 'black neck'—a derogatory term applied to UVF members by rival terror gangs, especially the UDA. It wasn't the first time lies about me had been printed in this publication, which put our staff, and myself, in peril.

But this particular piece could have got me killed.

———

Conducting interviews face-to-face with terrorist Godfathers was part and parcel of what many journalists, both local and from other parts, did during the Troubles. Getting threats from them, face-to-face, was not.

The most in-your-face threat I ever got was from Billy 'King Rat' Wright. And that wasn't just directed at me, it was directed at everyone in the *Sunday World* and everyone connected with it. It is chronicled in detail in my previous book, *Godfathers*. Others are reported in this book, like the INLA drugs dealer who told me he was going to get a gun to shoot me after we went head-to-head in a downtown Belfast bar.

Strangely enough, however, there are other Godfathers whom I have interviewed, sometimes in places of their choosing, where they were surrounded by notorious members of their mob, who have never threatened me. And one of them is perhaps the most notorious of all: Johnny 'Mad Dog' Adair. I have met and interviewed him many times, and not once, even though on occasions flanked by a horde of his 'heavies', has he threatened me.

Once, even, he told everyone else to leave the room—at the back of a UDA prisoners'-aid premises on the Shankill Road—and we sat facing each other. He was dressed in a black suit, white shirt, and black tie. It was a Saturday morning and he said he was going to a funeral. After the first question, I thought it was going to be mine.

Adair had requested the meeting, spurred by a series of stories we had been running about him being a big-time drug-dealer, and a drug-user—in his case steroids for bodybuilding.

He pulled a chair up tight and close. He turned it around, the back facing me, straddled the seat, put his arms over the back, and said: 'Your paper's making allegations about me. I'm no longer a paramilitary. I'm out of jail now. I'm a community worker…'

So I asked him, straight, eyeball-to-eyeball: 'Are you a drug-dealer?'

His answer to that was not even a one-liner. It was one word: 'No.'

'Do you take drugs?'

'No.'

'Do you inject steroids?'

'No.'

But I wasn't letting him away with the point-blank denials. I went at him, saying local people were citing him and his lower Shankill C Company as a drug-running cartel.

Again, he denied that, and a flotilla of supplementary questions the whole way through. At times, a stare as cold as the metal casing on the bullet he held between thumb and index finger came my way.

But no threat. In fact, from him, no threat at any time. And he continued to talk to us even when he was exiled in, first, England, and then, latterly, in the Scottish seaside town of Troon.

But at the end of this interview, which he had requested, he wanted to talk about a threat: to him, not to us. He had been holding that bullet between his thumb and index finger for a reason. He said it had been sent to him in the post that morning. He even produced the envelope, addressed to himself, from the inside pocket of the black, silk-lined Hugo Boss funeral suit he was wearing.

There was a note inside, saying the next bullet would not be put in an envelope, it would be put in his head. But he said he didn't believe it was from the IRA. He said he believed it was from within the ranks of the organisation in which he had risen to the rank of 'brigadier', the UDA.

This was the first sign that the UDA Inner Council were moving to dump Adair and drive his supporters in the rump of C Company out of Ulster, and across the Irish Sea. Adair didn't see that coming at the time. But then, he could be blinded to other facts as well. Like the cold fact, behind his cold stare, that he was indeed a drug-dealer and drug-user—one of the first of the paraMafia Godfathers, along with Jim 'Doris Day' Gray and the Shoukri brothers, to line the UDA's, and their own, coffers from the evil drugs trade.

So 'Mad Dog' never, personally, put the bite on me, or us, even when he sided with the LVF to spark the bitter internecine feud with the UVF in 2002 which was to claim eight lives in just a couple of months.

And neither did the Milltown cemetery murderer Michael Stone, later to hit the world headlines again in 2007 for trying to storm the Stormont Assembly, single-handed.

That was seven years after he'd been let out of the Maze jail under the early-release clause of the Good Friday Agreement. He had been sentenced in 1989 to a mammoth 684 years behind bars for six murders.

But in spite of his 'mass murderer' label, Stone had a sense of humour. I know, I interviewed him face-to-face. I know there should have been nothing to laugh about. But he was always disarmingly straight in dealing with the hardball questions fired at him after his release. And not least about two bids he made to murder the now Stormont Deputy First Minister, Martin McGuinness, in McGuinness's native town of Derry, before he tried again, and failed, at the gun-and-grenade attack at Milltown cemetery at the funeral of the Gibraltar Three in Belfast on 16 March 1988.

In a lengthy letter he posted to my wife, Lindy, at the *Belfast Telegraph* the day before he had the brainstormer which led him to try to storm Stormont, he admitted he was again trying to kill Martin McGuinness, and, in a re-run of Milltown, to murder Sinn Féin President Gerry Adams.

Stone's latest solo terror attack occurred on Friday 24 November 2006, and was thwarted by brave civilian security guards who trapped Stone in the main revolving door at the Assembly building, as pictures flashed around the world.

The next day, Saturday 25 November, Stone was escorted into a heavily guarded court by armed police. He faced five attempted murder charges, with Adams and McGuinness again being cited as his targets, along with terrorist weapons and explosives charges.

The letter to Lindy dominated the *Telegraph* front page, and a cascade of columns inside the following Monday. Father-of-nine Stone, then aged fifty-one, was to claim later that he was carrying out an act of 'performance art'. He was, of course, an artist, of sorts. He had taken up painting while in jail. And it was in that context, literally, that I was to brush up against his sense of humour.

I'd been present at the first Press conference Stone staged after he got out of jail on 24 July 2000. That, too, was held in the heart of Jim Gray's 'turf'. Gray was actually there of course, along with his cronies. But they knew better than to do anything with the world's Press there, and banks of TV cameras and newspaper photographers thronging both the Press conference inside, and the road outside.

But there was a bit of a spat when one of his heavies tried to censor a question put by a hack. The Press weren't standing for that, and made it known. But Stone himself intervened, through the man running the Press conference, and made it clear he would field any questions that were put to him.

The one I asked him was to hit the headlines the next day. There was a stony silence—to use an apt pun—when I asked Michael Stone if, now that he was out of jail, the war was over. After a pause, he said that for him, it was.

That was a big statement coming from him at the time and I believe it was later to lead to tension between him and Gray. Indeed, at one stage, there were rumours that Gray had ordered his hoods to give Stone a beating. That was one of the reasons Stone asked to see me. He wanted to give me an interview to 'set the record straight' about that rumour, among other things.

By this stage, he had taken up painting and was working out of a studio way at the back of the huge loyalist Ballybeen estate in East Belfast: a UDA stronghold, if ever there was one and a hideaway where the IRA would have the utmost difficulty in finding him, even if, as he repeatedly told me, he expected to be shot by the Provos with his own gun. (That is, one of the two weapons he had been firing at Milltown cemetery, and had been recovered by the mob of furious mourners who chased him as he tried to make his escape on the nearby M1 Motorway.)

So I went to meet Stone along with another *Sunday World* colleague and friend. We had been in many tight ends, got the job done, and got out of them. But this Saturday morning, using directions supplied by Stone, we arrived at the Ballybeen studio, to find a mob of minders there to greet us.

Now, at this stage, long before they, too, fell out with Jim Gray, his 'turf' as East Belfast Brigadier extended to here, too. They didn't fancy the *Sunday World*. There was a gaggle of growlers, until Stone himself came out to greet us.

The photographer snapped away, taking pictures not only of Stone doing an interview, but also of the backdrop of his studio and his paintings (in newspaper terms, to add 'colour' to the story).

Off the record, he told me what he really thought of Gray, seeing the writing on the wall for 'Doris' long before Gray could see it for himself.

Stone stressed that whatever else he was, he was not into drugs, and despised Gray and others in the UDA for dealing in them. He also hammered 'Mad Dog' Adair in the interview. But then again, he had told me before that he had fallen out with Adair in jail, and had even once offered to meet him 'outside' when both were behind bars, to have a digging match.

But this time, in the seclusion of his Ballybeen converted-shop studio, Stone said he was aware of the rumours that he had been given 'a kicking' on the orders of Gray. He denied that. He said that a lot of people were now noticing how difficult it was for him to walk. He was using a walking stick, but he maintained that was a result of the agony he was suffering with a 'bad back'.

He said his back had been badly injured when the mourners chasing him in his flight from Milltown cemetery caught up with him and gave him a pummelling before police arrived to rescue him. He said it was getting worse: much worse. Thus the bad limp and the use of the walking stick.

Stone denied, emphatically, that he had been 'rompered' on the orders of Gray and the interview over, I went outside. At least our car was still sitting there. And it wasn't sitting on bricks, with the wheels removed, neither was it a smoking, burnt-out shell. But the 'growlers' were still milling about.

Stone said he would accompany us to the car. I didn't demur. But then, halfway to the car, parked fifty yards from the front door of his studio, he stopped and said: 'Go ahead on, I'll be back.'

I knew him better than to think he'd leave us to be ambushed by 'the boys' still standing there as his minders. At least, I hoped I did…

But a couple of seconds later, he hobbled back to us, without the walking stick, but carrying a painting of the topless torso of a woman. Painted in oil and acrylic on wood, it was semi-abstract. The message wasn't. The woman's right forearm transformed into the shape of a snake's body, her right hand into a serpent's head. And in the centre of her own head was painted an apple, with a bite out of it.

Adam and Eve, in the Garden of Eden. And the title of the work? 'Temptation'. The front of the painting was signed 'M.S. 97'. On the back was a piece of white paper, signed 'Michael Stone 1997' (obviously done while he was still in jail, hence painted on wood rather than canvas) accompanied by a fingerprint, just like the cops take when arresting a suspect. I didn't ask then, but I was told later that the black ink finger-print was of the index finger on Stone's right hand. His trigger finger.

Anyway, I'm standing there when Stone hirples back out to us with the painting in a black frame. Without saying a word, he goes to hand it to me. I'm standing with my hands in my trouser pockets. I don't move. He gestures towards me to take the painting, again. Again, I don't move.

Then he looks me straight in the eyes. He's got those kind of Jimmy-Galway-the-flautist eyes, dancing in his head. He's smiling broadly. He says to me: 'I know what you want to tell me to do with this painting, McDowell.'

I stay schtum, hoping the silence doesn't lead the lamb to the slaughter.

He's still smiling. He says: 'You want to tell me to stick it up my arse, don't you?'

Again, I say nothing. And he's almost chuckling as he turns to someone else and says: 'Here, you put it in the boot of his car.' So, don't ask me how, but the painting ends up in the boot of the car.

But don't ask me where it is now. Because my answer would be: 'I can't tell you for security reasons.' Well, that's true, and accurate, given what this book's about, isn't it? But it's more likely to be in a loo, than the Louvre...

21 | 'FINGERED'

Michael Stone's fingerprint on the back of a painting is one thing. Being 'fingered'—having the finger pointed at you in public and being threatened—is quite another. That has happened to me many times. And while the police warning notices still come as a bit of a dunt it is the unexpected incident coming out of the blue, usually accompanied by blue and foul language, that can cause a bigger jolt.

These situations usually arise when gangs of terrorists, or their teenage supporters, are hunting in packs. When they're on their way to a football match, or they're 'down the town', cruising, just looking for trouble, and looking for someone to pick on.

Many times, that has been me. It's one of the reasons we don't—we can't—use public transport. You never know who's going to be on the bus, or train.

Increasingly, in the wake of 'peace' arriving—these boys are deserting the old stomping grounds of their own turf where they previously felt safe, and had 'control', or thought they had, for town, where they feel safer, especially in numbers. When you run into a team of these youngsters, the verbals can start to fly. It's very difficult, when under a barrage of insults in public, to keep your hands in your pockets, especially when the threat arises in the most innocuous and unexpected of places, like when you're out with your wife for a bit of grub, and there's a 'team', fired up on booze, at another table, who suddenly get enough in them to start slabbering at you.

'What about the Sunday Billy Liar?' is one of the lesser insults slung on such occasions.

Sometimes, it is best to just ignore it, and hope that the management really do as the sign on the door says and reserve the right to serve them any more drink, and also ask them to leave. Or, preferably, have them thrown out by the door staff.

But sometimes, you just have to take it… so far. And then you and your wife or the friends you are with feel it is appropriate, and safer, to leave yourselves.

And then there are the other times when things happen so randomly, so quickly, that you simply can't bite back on your tongue. One example out of many illustrates the point. I cite this not because it was a huge story about bombs or bullets or real bogeymen, but about how those who work for the paper always produce a product which lives on the cutting edge and how we live on the cutting edge ourselves.

It all started with something relatively mundane in Belfast, or Derry, or Armagh… or anywhere else in Northern Ireland. A riot.

It erupted on the night of Thursday, 1 September 2005, less than half a mile from the ornate and towering back gates of Belfast City Hall. The location: the junction of the Ormeau Road and Cromac Street overshadowed by the red brick walls of the old town gasworks. The participants: a Catholic mob from the Market district of the city, versus a Protestant mob from nearby Donegall Pass. The catalyst: well, the use of the word 'versus' in the previous paragraph is apt. Because this riot broke out over sport.

The rival groups, mainly boys and youths, went to war on the streets over the flying of flags celebrating a run of success enjoyed by a local GAA football team supported by people from the Market area. They'd put up the orange and black flags of St Malachy's GAA club in celebration, but the loyalists from Donegall Pass interpreted that as provocation. They tried putting up flags of their own on lamp posts flanking their patch.

Rival crowds gathered at what had become a traditional 'interface' during The Troubles. A riot ensued. Police rushed from nearby Donegall Pass police station to try to quell it. Eventually they did. But not before tens of thousands of pounds worth of damage to cars and property had been wreaked. Miraculously, in the mayhem, no one was seriously injured.

But by Sunday we had captured, literally, a bizarre but brutal picture. The photograph captured a teenager taking part in the riot with something like a hospital-issue crutch in his hand. But on closer examination, the freelance photographer who had snapped a series of images of the same teenage rioter noticed that what was meant to be a medical aid for a sick or injured person, had in fact been turned into a potentially lethal weapon. The rubber stopper at the end of the crutch where it touches the ground had been removed and a sharpened rod of steel—in effect, a spear—had been inserted up the aluminium shaft of the crutch.

And, using a scything movement with his left arm, the rioter was launching the spear. A police officer told us: 'If it had hit someone, it could have killed them.'

We splashed on the front page with the picture, headlining it 'LETHAL WEAPON'.

Inside, I wrote that this incident had taken place *seven years* after the signing of the Good Friday Agreement, pointing out that it was happening 'in an alleged time of peace, when the Bible says that weapons should be beaten into ploughshares.' I added: 'Instead, we have incidents like this where a hospital crutch is turned into a potentially lethal weapon.'

We also ran a banner headline over Pages 2 and 3 inside screaming 'SPEAR OF HATE', with more pictures of the spear hurler—he came from the Market area—plus the scene of devastation after the riot.

All of that appeared on Sunday, 4 September 2005. The following Tuesday I was approached in Belfast city centre by three men. It was obvious to me afterwards that they had been tracking my movements over lunchtime. They came up behind me. Without any preamble, one warned me: 'Don't be publishing any more of them [sic] f*****g pictures.'

I copped immediately what he was on about. Sunday's lead story and pictures. The youth in the pictures had been clearly identifiable. There must have been 'heat' from the police in trying to lift him. We were getting the blame—again. And these three arseholes—or one of them anyway—could well have been related to the spear thrower: or others taking part in the riot.

Your men didn't even break pace. They just walked on. And instead of ignoring them, I rose to the bait. I told them what to do with themselves in language that was as colourful as the pictures of the wee hood with the 'killer crutch'. I might even have gone as far as to tell them that if they brought the crutch to me, I would help them stick it where it belonged.

They hesitated and turned, as if to come back. But I wasn't budging. There's only so much s**t they can shovel at you. And as I've said, it's especially hard to take when you're least expecting it.

However, a couple of men standing close to me, good lads, twigged to the tension crackling between me and the three strangers. 'You all right, big McDowell?' one of them, who can handle himself, asked. The three interlopers took note. If they wanted to do anything, the odds were now even: three on three.

They looked at the two men who would answer any Mayday call I made. Then the one who had done the slabbering in the first place looked at me. 'Just don't be publishing any more of them pictures,' he repeated, before walking on.

However, as he went, I reminded him: 'If you've got any more of them on you, give me a call. We pay good money for them…' He uttered a profanity, but he, and his two mates, kept walking, instead of talking.

So that's how an offbeat picture, even if the angle is still street violence, can literally 'spearhead' a threat, however unexpectedly. Although that particular story was to have a humorous corollary.

Our colleagues over in the *Sunday Life*—they are our 'opposition', even though we are both owned by the Independent Media group and are, technically at least, 'sister' papers—thought it was a bizarre lead for us to splash on. So they mocked up an image of me on their computers. They substituted my face for that of Bobby Sands on the famous mural at the side of Sinn Féin headquarters on the Falls Road. And they inserted in front of it a 'sniper' in balaclava and battle fatigues brandishing not an Armalite or AK 47—but a crutch!

Very funny, lads. We had a good giggle over it over a few pints when they presented me with the mocked-up pic.

But we had the last laugh. The *Sunday World*, with that 'LETHAL WEAPON' pic and headline on the cover, racked up one of the biggest sales of 2005.

And it still goes to show that going for an angle on a story—no matter how bizarre it may seem—often pays off where it matters: with the punters who pay for newspapers, not just with the pencil pushers who write for them.

But to return to the stories which can spark threats from way out left of field, and where you least expect them, it is Saturday morning, 2 February 2008. Councillor Bert Wilson, the Chairman of Omagh District Council, comes on the phone. He tells us that sex ogre Eamon Foley, convicted of the brutal rape of a local pensioner, is on the loose again—and back living in the area where he committed the heinous crime.

Forty-eight-year-old Foley is out after serving half of a sixteen-year sentence for the rape of ninety-one-year-old Mary Anne McLaughlin. The defenceless old lady died just four weeks after the depraved sex assault.

Throughout his time in the remote Magilligan jail in north County Derry unrepentant Foley protested his innocence and tried to mount a campaign from behind bars to prove it. He even once made contact with me, through a third party. He offered to get me a pass to the jail to visit him. He said he would prove his innocence. Against my instincts, I agreed to go and see him.

I drove to Magilligan on a bleak, rainswept winter's afternoon.

Some of the prison officers there knew me as soon as I checked in for the visit. They asked me who I was in to visit. Then they asked me if I was right in the head.

They'd already made up their mind about Foley. It didn't take me long to make up my mind about him, either. As soon as he walked into the visitor's room, I knew: it wasn't me who wasn't right in the head. It was him, for still putting up the charade that he was innocent and for thinking he could get a grizzled oul' hack like me to buy into his sick fantasy. The way he walked, the bead of sweat on his brow, the clammy hand-shake which followed a very stilted introduction: as soon as I clapped eyes on him, I knew. Foley was guilty of the terrible sin he had committed in raping that gentle old woman.

Worse, there were people in that communal visiting area, relatives of other inmates, whom I knew. They looked at me meeting Foley and could hardly believe their eyes.

I was out of there as fast as I could extract myself. And that was the last time I had heard of Foley, until the phone call from Bert Wilson. 'People are up in arms around here,' he told me. 'Folk, especially the elderly living alone, are afraid to sleep in their beds at night.'

Bert pinpointed, on the phone, the house where Foley was hiding out. He gave me the number of the isolated farmhouse off the Woodlands Road at Bentrim, near the village of Gortin in the Glen, fifteen miles from Omagh.

I had a lot on that morning. But I told courageous Councillor Wilson that I'd either be visiting Foley with our photographer, Conor McCaughley, no stranger to gutsy assignments, or one of our reporters would.

Big Richard Sullivan, the deputy Editor, came in. I told him what the score was. I also told him that after what amounted to me snubbing Foley on the Magilligan jail visit it was unlikely that if I doorstepped him, he would talk to me. The big lad immediately volunteered to go with Conor. They could make it in an hour-and-a-half from the Belfast office.

But Gortin Glen is a remote location, with exact addresses notoriously hard to find. So I phoned Bert Wilson back. I asked him if he would go with our boys and pinpoint the house for them.

Like big Sully, he agreed, without hesitation. He met our lads outside Omagh, and took them to the house where Foley was holed up.

Bert, in that sense, was invaluable. Police were on duty at the entrance to the skinny wee road where the house was situated. But Councillor Wilson knew the area like the back of not one, but both his hands; he took the lads round a labyrinth of back roads and they landed in the yard of the house where Foley was staying before he, or the police on duty up the road, knew about it.

But even then it took another reporter's ruse for Foley to let them in and talk to them. While they were on their way to Gortin, another local from the area had phoned looking for me. He said that Foley might want to talk, but not that day. However, he would want to give his story to the *Sunday World*.

He gave me his name. I said that was OK, and for him to give us the nod if Foley ever decided to give us an interview. Then I phoned the boys on the road. I gave Richard Sullivan the name of the punter who'd phoned me offering the interview 'at some stage in the future.' We agreed he should use that name if Foley was showing any resistance to talking when Sully knocked at the door.

As it happened, the mention of the name of the other boy who had phoned me—a supporter of the Foley 'I'm innocent' cause—literally turned the key in the door. Sully and Conor were in. But not before Foley frisked them for guns—in case they were there to shoot him, told Conor to leave his camera behind the door in the hallway and then proved that a death threat can come from even the most unexpected quarter when he stunned them by declaring: 'Take my picture, even from the back, and I'll put a bullet in the back of your head!'

And that wasn't all. He told Conor: 'You can follow me around with a camera if you like, just don't let me catch up with me at any time. You can ask anybody in Castlederg what I'll do to you.' Don't forget, Castlederg is where his hapless and frail rape victim, Mary Anne McLaughlin—aged 91—lived. So much for the 'innocent' Mr Foley…

Still, like anybody who has ever threatened us, he got his pay-back on the front page the next morning. The only paper to have tracked him down to his lair that Saturday, we put him on the front page, picture and all—including a picture of the house where he was holed up. The headline on the front page, in big, bold capital letters screamed:

GOTCHA!

The sub-head, beside a blown-up mugshot of Foley, ran: We track down granny rapist who warns us: 'I'll put a bullet in you.' And the front page write-off, billed EXCLUSIVE by Richard Sullivan read:

> The *Sunday World* yesterday tracked down sex ogre Eamon Foley to his Gortin Glen bolt-hole in County Tyrone.
>
> But when we confronted 48-year-old Foley—convicted of raping pensioner Mary Anne McLaughlin, aged 91—he THREATENED us!
>
> After inviting us into his farmhouse hide-away he bluntly told us: 'Take my picture and I'll put a bullet in your head.'
>
> EVIL PERVERT EXPOSED: See Pages 4&5.

Aye, long runs the fox, as they say. But Foley had tried to fox me once, in jail. I didn't run with his story of 'innocence' then, and when he threatened our lads, he found he couldn't outfox us a second time either. 'Foley the fox', and his secret bolthole were unearthed on the front page of the *Sunday World* on Sunday 3 February 2008.

And he was living proof that we were still open to death threats ten years after the signing of the Good Friday Agreement, which was supposed to bring peace to Ulster, to Ireland... and to us!

POSTSCRIPT

The frank reporting which is the hallmark of the *Sunday World* newspaper is reflected in the words of one Frank Sinatra—we did it our way—and we continue to do it, distinctively, our way. In spite of the murder of Marty, the torching of the office, the threats that came, and still come.

Still, we go on exposing the bogeymen and women, the Godfathers and Godmothers, who would hold this society, this country, to ransom: not for reasons of political ideology, but in order to line their own pockets. And we continue to chart the morphing of the paramilitaries who once terrorised this country into the paraMafia who now prostitute it.

There is no more stark evidence of this then the two 'main men' profiled in this book. The Mummy's Boys; the Shoukris. Theirs is a shocking tale of greed, violence and intimidation, but they are by no means the only gangsters still stalking our society. There are those on the loyalist side who say they walk in the shadow of the men who fought at the Somme in 1916. There are those on the republican side who say they walk in the shadow of the men who fought at the GPO in Dublin in 1916. But, quite frankly, those who triggered and took part in the torrid, terror-ridden and savage sectarian trough in our history euphemistically labelled the Troubles, couldn't lace the boots of the brave men from throughout Ireland who died in the First World War.

Both sides are fooling themselves. Shooting men in the back of the head as they went for a walk with their wives, planting indiscriminate car bombs which caused the mass murder of men, women and children did not constitute a 'war'. Quite the opposite: these were war crimes.

None of these people will ever win the Nobel Peace Prize. One who did was Theodore Roosevelt, President of the United States from 1901–1909. He said, 'There are two kinds of success. One is the rare kind that comes to the person who has the power to do what no one else has the power to do. That is genius. But the average person who wins what we call success is not a genius. That person is a man or woman who has merely the ordinary qualities that they share with their fellows, but has developed these ordinary qualities to a more than ordinary degree.'

Humbly, I would dare to suggest that the men and women who work for this newspaper, in the face of the adversity which I have written about in this book—are Roosevelt's people. I salute them, both as colleagues and as friends.